LUMIÈRE *Light*

ROB FEENIE & MARNIE COLDHAM

with contributions from
MARCIA KURBIS, CHRIS STEARNS *and* NIC NEUMAN
photography by JOHN SHERLOCK

foreword by **DANIEL BOULUD**

RECIPES *from the* TASTING BAR

LUMIÈRE *Light*

DOUGLAS & McINTYRE
Vancouver/Toronto/Berkeley

Douglas & McIntyre
2323 Quebec Street, Suite 201
Vancouver, British Columbia
Canada v5t 4s7
www.douglas-mcintyre.com

National Library of Canada
Cataloguing in Publication Data
Feenie, Rob, 1965–

    Lumière light : recipes from the tasting bar /
Rob Feenie and Marnie Coldham; with a
foreword by Daniel Boulud.

    ISBN 1-55054-973-1

    1. Lumière (Restaurant) 2. Cookery—
British Columbia—Vancouver. I. Coldham,
Marnie, 1972– II. Title.
TX945.5.L84F42 2003   641.5′09711′33
C2003-910571-7

Library of Congress Cataloging-in-Publication data
is available

Editing by Saeko Usukawa
Jacket and interior design by Peter Cocking
with Jessica Sullivan
Food styling by Nathan Fong
Printed and bound in Canada by Friesens
Printed on acid-free paper
Distributed in the U.S. by Publishers Group West

The publisher gratefully acknowledges the
financial support of the Canada Council for the
Arts, the British Columbia Arts Council, and the
Government of Canada through the Book Publishing
Industry Development Program (BPIDP) for its
publishing activities.

Contents

When Rob Feenie mentioned his new cookbook to me, I accepted his invitation to write the foreword before even seeing the manuscript. To begin with, I like what Rob Feenie does. I agree with his philosophy of what food should be and why one cooks. I respect his work ethic and his dedication to his craft. I appreciate his commitment to use only the most excellent of seasonal ingredients and to constantly challenge himself by creating new dishes. I have never had the pleasure of dining at Lumière, but I have heard only good things about it from my patrons and fellow chefs. And, last but not least, I thought that his first cookbook, *Rob Feenie Cooks at Lumière,* was fabulous. When I received this manuscript, it was nice to see that my instincts had been correct.

The recipes in this book encompass a broad spectrum of original ideas that show-case Rob's passion for food and his creativity. He demonstrates how a chef can pack the maximum of taste into a dish but keep it simple. The recipes range from those like Caramelized Endive, Blue Cheese and Walnut Risotto, which illus-trates Rob's dynamic and vibrant cooking style, to those like his Four-Cheese Maca-roni, which is downright homey but in a way that only a world-class chef could devise. Throughout this cookbook, one thing remains constant: no matter what original twists the recipe contains, there is always an underlying thread of classicism.

All professionally trained chefs start with the same basics of classic French cuisine. Some make this cuisine their be-all and end-all and spend years perfecting it. Others use it as a base to which they add personal touches. In Rob's case, this has meant the addition of nature's bounty indigenous to Canada, the flavours of all the immigrant population of his beloved Vancouver and various tastes picked up along his travels. From this interesting combination of French and Asian (to name but two major influences) comes the cui-sine for which Lumière has garnered many awards. Sake and Maple Marinated Sablefish with Hijiki-Soy Sauce or Rob's take on a classic such as Shepherd's Pie—these recipes are a perfect illustration of Rob and the very personal cooking that he is now famous for.

I hope that you enjoy this book and the glimpse of this gifted chef as much as I did.

*I*nitially, we built the Tasting Bar at Lumière to hold the spillover of patrons waiting to be seated in our main dining room. Soon after it opened, however, it became apparent that many of our guests enjoyed—and some even preferred—the cool atmosphere of the bar. I, too, was drawn to its soothing ambiance. For me, it became a place to relax, recharge and restock.

The room soon took on a personality of its own, inspiring me to create a separate à la carte menu, one that reflects the Tasting Bar as an extension of Lumière while also defining it as an entity unto itself.

After an evening of work, I would find myself craving nothing more than a simple pasta or sandwich. I wanted a dish that was gratifying, yet not as involved as the numerous courses that pass through my kitchen during the evening. I wanted traditional bistro food with a unique, modern twist. With help from my kitchen staff, I developed a menu that offered simplicity and comfort while still possessing that defining Lumière touch. And thus the Tasting Bar philosophy was born.

The title of this book, *Lumière Light,* reflects a more casual cooking style that is accessible to every home cook. From the beef dip sandwich to the squash and mascarpone ravioli, basic recipes evolve into dishes that are sophisticated yet comforting. This book will challenge your culinary skills and spark your creativity while never being too intimidating.

Making this food leaves me with a simple satisfaction. I hope the recipes in this book do the same for you.

ROB FEENIE

Melon with Shaved Foie Gras / *4*

Truffled Raw Milk Camembert with
Roasted Figs and Brioche / *5*

Mushroom Torte with
Warm Soy Vinaigrette / *6*

Deep-fried Brandade
with Black Olive Tapenade / *10*

Appetizers

MELON WITH SHAVED *Foie Gras*

*C*hef Michel Jacob has had a great impact on me and my career. Years ago, he sent me to meet a good friend of his, Johnny Letzer, who owns a small little restaurant in the middle of Strasbourg called Au Boeuf Mode. A year ago, after doing a dinner for the thirtieth anniversary of Relais Gourmand, I visited Johnny again. He had some beautiful Charentais melons from southern France that he used for this dish. All you do is scoop out the inside of the melon and put it together with a little bit of balsamic, some Pineau de Charentes, shavings of chilled foie gras and some fleur de sel. That's it. It is a very simple yet sophisticated dish.

Pineau de Charentes is a sweet aperitif made by adding one-year-old Cognac to grape juice that is on the verge of becoming wine. *Serves 4*

4 Charentais melons or cantaloupes (each 1 lb.)
3 Tbsp. extra-virgin olive oil
¼ tsp. fleur de sel
¼ tsp. cracked black pepper
¼ lobe raw foie gras, chilled
4 Tbsp. 25-year-old balsamic vinegar or balsamic glaze (page 126)
½ cup Pineau de Charentes

TO MAKE: Cut off the top ½ to 1 inch of melons (or cantaloupes), then scoop out and discard seeds. Scoop out inside flesh, leaving ¼ inch thickness on rind. Place melon flesh in a bowl and season with extra-virgin olive oil, a little fleur de sel and cracked black pepper to taste.

TO ASSEMBLE: Place seasoned melon pieces back inside shells.

Use a vegetable peeler to shave off thin pieces from the chilled foie gras and place inside melons. Work quickly, as foie gras will soften and make this process very difficult.

Sprinkle the rest of the fleur de sel and cracked black pepper inside melons. Drizzle 1 tablespoon of aged balsamic vinegar (or balsamic glaze) inside each melon. Serve Pineau des Charentes on the side, for diners to pour inside melons according to individual taste.

TRUFFLED RAW MILK *Camembert* WITH

ROASTED FIGS AND *Brioche*

This is something my good friend Johnny Letzer in Strasbourg made for us at his house one Sunday afternoon. It is unbelievable how the truffle flavour infuses and melds into the Camembert. Of course, it wouldn't be the same without the roasted figs and brioche. This dish can be served on its own with a bottle of wine or as a beautiful decadent cheese course to end a meal. *Serves 6 to 8*

BRIOCHE (page 128)

CAMEMBERT
1 lb. whole round of Camembert cheese
⅔ cup mascarpone
⅔ cup heavy cream, whipped to soft peaks
3 Tbsp. chopped black truffle
2 tsp. white truffle oil
½ tsp. sea salt
⅛ tsp. freshly ground white pepper

FIGS
6 to 8 fresh figs
1 cup Japanese plum wine
1 cup fresh orange juice
¼ cup wildflower or regular honey

TO MAKE BRIOCHE: Make a loaf according to instructions and set aside.

CAMEMBERT: Use a serrated knife to carefully slice camembert in half horizontally, to make two rounds.

Gently whisk mascarpone to soften in a bowl. Fold in whipped cream. Add truffle, truffle oil, sea salt and white pepper. Spread mascarpone mixture evenly on the cut side of one half of the camembert. Place the other half of the camembert, cut side down, on top of filling. Wrap tightly in plastic wrap and refrigerate for at least a day.

FIGS: Preheat the oven to 350°F.

Use a paring knife to score the bottom of each fig and place in a baking dish. Set aside 3 tablespoons of plum wine. Combine the rest of the plum wine, orange juice and honey in a bowl, then pour over figs. Roast in the oven for 8 to 10 minutes, or until figs are soft. Remove figs from the baking dish and set aside on a plate. Pour liquid from the baking dish into a saucepan on medium heat. Cook to reduce liquid, stirring occasionally, until syrupy. Pour syrup over figs to glaze them.

TO ASSEMBLE: Preheat the oven to 350°F.

Place Camembert on a plate and cut into 6 or 8 wedges, depending on the number you are serving. Allow to sit until it reaches room temperature.

Place figs in a baking dish, add the 3 tablespoons of plum wine and reheat in the oven for about 3 minutes, or until warmed through.

Cut brioche into slices ½-inch thick and place on a parchment-lined baking sheet. Toast in the oven for 3 to 5 minutes, or until lightly browned.

Place a wedge of Camembert on each plate. Place a warm fig to the side of the cheese and spoon a little glaze over the fig. Arrange toasted brioche on a side plate.

Mushroom TORTE WITH *Warm Soy* VINAIGRETTE

I love mushrooms, and if I could, I would put them into every dish. I also love the warm vinaigrette, as not only does it add a tasty element to this dish but it is so versatile that it can be served with anything. You can experiment and use whatever mushrooms are your favourites. *Serves 4*

FILLING

2 Tbsp. olive oil
2 Tbsp. unsalted butter
2 shallots, peeled and thinly sliced
4 cups wild mushrooms (oyster, chanterelle, morel), cut into uniform pieces
2 Tbsp. Madeira
2 Tbsp. sherry vinegar
4 Tbsp. heavy cream
1 Tbsp. finely chopped fresh tarragon

PASTRY

1 pkg. frozen puff pastry, thawed
Nonstick cooking spray
2 egg yolks
2 Tbsp. cold water

VINAIGRETTE

4 Tbsp. light soy sauce
2 Tbsp. rice vinegar
2 Tbsp. fresh lemon juice
8 Tbsp. olive oil

1 head frisée, washed and trimmed, for garnish

TO MAKE FILLING: Heat olive oil and butter in two large frying pans on medium-high heat. Add shallots and sauté for 2 minutes, or until soft and translucent. Add mushrooms and sauté, stirring occasionally, for about 10 minutes, or until they have released and reabsorbed their natural juices. Season with salt and freshly ground white pepper to taste. Decrease the heat to medium, then add Madeira and sherry vinegar; cook for 2 minutes. Add cream and tarragon, then continue to cook until cream is reduced and nicely coats mushrooms. Remove from the stove and allow to cool. Cover and refrigerate until ready to use.

PASTRY: Divide puff pastry into 8 portions. On a lightly floured surface, roll out each portion of pastry to make a circle 5 ½ to 6 inches in diameter, ⅛ inch thick. Coat the insides of four individual ovenproof molds (3 inches in diameter and 2 inches high) with nonstick cooking spray.

Place a piece of pastry inside each mold and press to ensure a good fit. Trim off and discard edges of pastry. Place pastry-lined molds in the freezer for 10 to 15 minutes. Remove from the freezer and fill with mushroom mixture.

Make an egg wash by whisking egg yolks with water in a bowl. Use half of the egg wash to brush one side of the remaining pieces of pastry. Place a piece of pastry, egg-washed side facing down, on top of each torte. Pinch pastry all around to seal the edges, then trim the pastry. Place tortes back in the freezer for 20 minutes.

TORTES: Preheat the oven to 350°F.

Remove mushroom tortes from the freezer and place on a baking sheet. Brush the remaining egg wash on the top of each and sprinkle with a little salt. Bake in the oven for about 5 minutes, or until light golden brown. Decrease the heat to 325°F and continue to bake for another 10 to 15 minutes, or until the tops are dark golden brown and puff pastry is cook thoroughly on the bottom. Remove from the oven and allow to cool.

When the tortes are cool, carefully remove them from the molds.

VINAIGRETTE: Combine light soy sauce, rice vinegar and lemon juice in a saucepan on medium-low heat. Bring to a simmer, then remove from the heat and whisk in olive oil. Season to taste with salt and freshly ground white pepper. Keep warm.

TO ASSEMBLE: Place a little frisée lettuce in the centre of each of four plates. Place a mushroom torte on top of each serving and drizzle warm soy vinaigrette around it.

Chrysanthemum Cocktail

2 oz. French (white) vermouth

1 oz. Benedictine

1 dash fresh lemon juice

Wedge of lemon, for garnish

. . .

Pour vermouth, Benedictine and lemon juice into a shaker full of cracked ice and shake well. Strain into a chilled cocktail glass. Garnish with a lemon wedge.

The 1930s signalled the twilight of a golden era for sea-borne passenger travel. Regal fleets plied their transatlantic routes in luxury. Foremost among these proud craft was the ss *Europa*. Harry Craddock, legendary Prohibition-era barman at London's Savoy Hotel Bar, tells us that the *Europa*'s American Bar served a specialty known as the Chrysanthemum Cocktail—a silken secret that became a favourite among its sea-legged patrons. We concur, but prefer to imbibe ours on dry land. This is a lighter drink that is perfect as a gentle start to the evening, or for occasions which necessitate moderation.

MIXING TIPS: Some recipes for the Chrysanthemum include a dash of anisette (like Pernod or Ricard). It makes a nice addition to the drink, but be sure to only add a drop or two, or the pastis will easily overwhelm the other flavours.

DEER-FRIED *Brandade* WITH BLACK OLIVE *Tapenade*

Traditional brandade is made with salt cod. Our rendition uses fresh ling cod, which makes the flavour a little milder. We've also added an extra step to make it a little bit different: deep-frying. Rolling pieces of brandade in crisp Japanese bread crumbs and deep-frying them creates a delicious contrast to the soft texture of the potato and cod. This can be served as an appetizer, but I think it also make an excellent hors d'oeuvre. *Serves 4 to 6*

TAPENADE

1 cup niçoise olives, pitted
1 anchovy fillet
3 Tbsp. capers, rinsed
3 cloves garlic, peeled
1 Tbsp. fresh lemon juice
2 Tbsp. finely chopped fresh Italian
   (flat-leaf) parsley
½ cup extra-virgin olive oil

BRANDADE

12 oz. Yukon Gold potatoes, skin on
1 cup milk, 2 per cent
¼ cup water
8 sprigs fresh thyme
1 bay leaf
9 white peppercorns
1 clove garlic, peeled and crushed
8 oz. ling cod, cut into 4 pieces
½ cup heavy cream
2 Tbsp. garlic purée (page 125)
4 Tbsp. extra-virgin olive oil
Peanut oil for deep-frying
3 to 4 cups panko (Japanese bread crumbs)

TO MAKE TAPENADE: Purée olives, anchovy, capers and garlic in a food processor or blender. Add lemon juice and parsley. Continue to pulse while slowly adding olive oil. (Place any extra tapenade in an airtight container; will keep in the refrigerator for up to 3 days.)

BRANDADE: Place potatoes, skin on, in a saucepan and add enough lightly salted water to cover. Bring to a boil on high heat, then decrease the heat to medium and simmer for 15 to 20 minutes, or until potatoes are fork-tender. Drain. Peel potatoes and put through a ricer or food mill. Keep warm.

In another saucepan, combine milk, water, thyme, bay leaf, peppercorns and garlic. Bring to a boil on medium heat. Add ling cod and simmer for 2 minutes. Remove from the heat and allow fish to cool in the poaching liquid for about 5 minutes.

In a small saucepan, bring cream just to a boil on medium heat. Remove from the heat and keep warm.

Remove fish from the poaching liquid. Place equal amounts (8 oz. of each) potatoes and cod in the bowl of a kitchen mixer with a paddle attachment. Mix on a low speed, slowly adding warm cream. Add garlic purée and extra-virgin olive oil. Season with salt and freshly ground white pepper. Allow to cool.

TO ASSEMBLE: Preheat peanut oil for deep-frying from 375°F to 400°F.

Roll brandade into small balls, using 1½ to 2 tablespoons for each. Then roll in panko and deep-fry until golden brown. Place on paper towels to absorb excess oil and sprinkle with a little salt.

Arrange deep-fried brandade to form a mound on a warmed plate, and place tapenade on the side.

Ahi Tuna Sashimi and Green Papaya
Salad with Chile-Lime Dressing / 15

Orange-glazed Duck Leg Salad / 16

Grilled Asparagus Salad with
Prosciutto, Parmigiano-Reggiano
and Balsamic Vinaigrette / 17

Duck Breast Salad with Vanilla-poached
Quince and Pomegranate / 18

Spicy Lemon Grass and
Seafood Soup / 23

Chicken Noodle Soup
with Garlic Croutons / 25

Shiitake Mushroom Cappuccino / 26

The Beef Dip with Hand-cut Fries
and a Micro Green Salad / 31

Calamari Sandwich / 34

Peking Duck Clubhouse / 36

Salads, Soups & Sandwiches

< AHI TUNA *Sashimi* AND GREEN PAPAYA SALAD
WITH *Chile-Lime* DRESSING

I have always been a fan of sashimi. The trick to this recipe is to get a centre cut of Grade-A Ahi tuna. It has a vibrant red colour, which alone is so beautiful you almost don't want to eat it. The green papaya is unripened, picked prematurely and bled to get rid of its white acidic juice. It adds a lovely texture to this dish, yet the flavour is subtle enough not to overpower the delicate taste of the fish. The Asian dressing adds the needed elements of spiciness and saltiness to complement the fish. The flavours are clean yet complex. You can serve it as an appetizer or as a main course. *Serves 4*

DRESSING

¼ cup fish sauce
¼ cup fresh lime juice
1 Tbsp. palm sugar (Asian food stores)
1-inch piece lemon grass, roughly chopped
¼ to ½ Thai chile, roughly chopped
Pinch of minced garlic
½ cup water

SALAD

2 tsp. dried shrimp
¼ cup water
½ cup julienned green papaya
1 Tbsp. julienned mint leaves
1 Tbsp. julienned cilantro leaves
1 Tbsp. julienned Thai basil leaves
4 Tbsp. toasted pine nuts
4 Tbsp. tomato concassé (page 124)
6 green beans, blanched and finely diced
8 slices Grade-A Ahi tuna loin (each 2-oz.), ¼-inch thick
¼ cup cilantro oil (page 125) for garnish

TO MAKE DRESSING: Place all dressing ingredients in a blender and process until smooth. Immediately strain through a fine-mesh sieve. Cover and refrigerate overnight to allow flavours to infuse.

SALAD: Combine dried shrimp and water in a saucepan on medium heat and bring to a boil. Remove from the heat and immediately strain through a fine-mesh sieve; discard liquid. Place drained shrimp on a paper towel to dry. Mince shrimp, place in a covered container and refrigerate until needed.

TO ASSEMBLE: In a bowl, mix together shrimp, green papaya, mint, cilantro, Thai basil, pine nuts, tomato concassé and green beans. Add ¼ cup of dressing and toss gently.

Place 2 slices of Ahi tuna in the centre of each of four large chilled plates. Drizzle cilantro oil around the outside of the tuna. Spoon 2 tablespoons of dressing over each serving. Divide salad and arrange on top of fish.

ORANGE-GLAZED *Duck Leg* SALAD

*D*uck confit. You can never have too much of it. And what goes better with duck than an orange sauce? This salad is very simple, very delicious and very classic, all at the same time. Rich, sweet and tangy. *Serves 4*

HOUSE VINAIGRETTE
1 tsp. Dijon mustard
4 ½ tsp. red wine vinegar
4 ½ tsp. sherry vinegar
½ tsp. dry sherry
½ cup grapeseed oil
1 tsp. fresh lemon juice

DUCK
1 cup fresh orange juice
½ cup Cointreau or Grand Marnier
1 cup dark chicken stock (page 120)
2 Tbsp. unsalted butter
4 duck legs and thighs confit (page 72)

6 cups mesclun

TO MAKE HOUSE VINAIGRETTE:
Whisk together mustard, red wine and sherry vinegars, and sherry in a stainless steel bowl. Whisking constantly, very slowly drizzle in grapeseed oil. Whisk in lemon juice. Season to taste with salt and freshly ground white pepper. Transfer to an airtight container until needed; will keep in the refrigerator for up to 1 week.

DUCK: Preheat the oven to 350°F.

Combine orange juice and Cointreau (or Grand Marnier) in a saucepan on medium-high heat and simmer, stirring occasionally, until reduced to a syrupy liquid. Add dark chicken stock and cook until reduced by half. Whisk in butter and keep warm.

Remove duck legs and attached thighs from fat, wiping off excess. Arrange them on a baking sheet and place in the oven for 10 to 15 minutes to heat through and to crisp skin. Remove from the oven and keep warm.

TO ASSEMBLE: Place mesclun in a bowl and toss with 6 to 8 tablespoons vinaigrette to lightly coat leaves. Season with a little salt and freshly ground white pepper and toss again.

Divide mesclun among four dinner plates. Place a warmed duck leg on top of each serving and spoon warm orange glaze over it.

GRILLED *Asparagus Salad* WITH PROSCIUTTO, PARMIGIANO-REGGIANO AND *Balsamic* VINAIGRETTE

I could eat this simple but perfect dish all year long, but it is best in the spring and the summer when asparagus is at its peak. The smokiness of the grilled asparagus, the saltiness of the prosciutto and Parmigiano, and the tart sweetness of the balsamic vinegar smoothed by the extra-virgin olive oil make for an absolutely delicious combination. *Serves 4*

VINAIGRETTE
1 shallot, peeled and finely chopped
1 tsp. honey
2 Tbsp. balsamic vinegar
6 Tbsp. extra-virgin olive oil

SALAD
2 lbs. green asparagus
4 Tbsp. extra-virgin olive oil
8 slices prosciutto
4 cups mesclun or other salad greens
Parmigiano-Reggiano (Parmesan cheese)
   for garnish

TO MAKE VINAIGRETTE: In a stainless steel bowl, combine shallot, honey and balsamic vinegar. Whisking continuously, slowly add olive oil until emulsified. Season to taste with salt and freshly ground white pepper. Cover and refrigerate until ready to use.

ASPARAGUS: Preheat the grill to medium-high heat.

Snap or cut off fibrous ends from asparagus. Bring a large saucepan of salted water to a boil. Blanch asparagus in boiling water for 1 minute, then immediately plunge into ice water to stop the cooking and to preserve colour. Place asparagus on a paper towel to dry.

In a stainless steel bowl, toss blanched asparagus with olive oil to coat (to prevent asparagus from sticking to the grill). Season to taste with salt and freshly ground white pepper. Grill asparagus for 2 to 3 minutes, turning on all sides. (The cooking time is short as asparagus is already partially cooked.)

TO ASSEMBLE: Divide asparagus among four warmed plates. Spoon vinaigrette over and around asparagus. Place 2 slices of prosciutto on top of each serving. Top with mesclun (or other salad greens) and drizzle with a little more vinaigrette. Use a vegetable peeler or a sharp knife to thinly slice Parmigiano-Reggiano into curls and place a few on top of each serving.

DUCK BREAST *Salad* WITH VANILLA-POACHED *Quince* AND POMEGRANATE >

Quince is a fruit that is not used much. It has a very bitter sharp flavour, so it's a good foil for the richness of duck. In this recipe, we poach it just the way you would pears, with a little bit of vanilla. This gives the quince a wonderful flavour.

My friend Joan Cross showed me a handy trick for seeding pomegranates with little or no mess. Simply use a knife to remove the outer skin of a pomegranate, then place it in a large bowl of cold water. Pull the sections of pomegranate apart so that you can separate the seeds more easily, all without staining your hands. *Serves 4*

DUCK
2 half breasts of duck, skin on
2 tsp. vegetable oil

QUINCE
1 vanilla bean, split and pulp scraped
1 cup water
¾ cup granulated sugar
1 tsp. fresh lemon juice
2 quince, peeled, ¼-inch dice

VINAIGRETTE
¾ cup pomegranate juice (specialty store)
¼ cup rice vinegar
2 Tbsp. fresh lemon juice
½ cup extra-virgin olive oil

SALAD
4 cups mesclun or other salad greens
¼ cup pomegranate seeds
1 smoked duck breast, julienned (optional)
Coarse sea salt for garnish

TO MAKE DUCK: Preheat the oven to 400°F.

Score skin of duck breasts to ensure even cooking. Season with salt and freshly ground white pepper. Heat vegetable oil in a large ovenproof frying pan on medium-high heat. Sear duck, skin side down, for 2 to 3 minutes. Pour off and discard fat from the pan. Place the pan in the oven. Roast for 4 to 5 minutes.

Remove from the oven, then pour off and discard excess fat. Turn duck over again, so skin side is up, and return to the oven for another 4 to 5 minutes for medium-rare, or until desired doneness. Remove from the oven and keep warm.

QUINCE: Combine vanilla bean pulp and pod, water, sugar and lemon juice in a saucepan. Bring to a boil on medium-high heat. Add quince and bring to a boil again. Remove from the heat and allow to cool. Use a slotted spoon to remove quince from poaching liquid; reserve quince and poaching liquid separately. Cover and refrigerate until needed.

VINAIGRETTE: Place pomegranate juice in a saucepan on medium heat and cook until reduced by half and syrupy. Transfer to a stainless steel bowl and allow to cool. Add rice vinegar, lemon juice and 2 tablespoons of the reserved quince poaching liquid. Slowly whisk in olive oil. Season to taste with salt and freshly ground white pepper.

TO ASSEMBLE: Gently toss together mesclun (or other salad greens), pomegranate seeds, quince and smoked duck (optional) with 3 to 5 tablespoons of vinaigrette, or enough to coat the greens. Season with salt and freshly ground white pepper.

Divide salad among four plates. Slice duck breasts and place equal amounts on top of greens for each serving. Sprinkle duck with a little coarse sea salt. Drizzle a little vinaigrette around the salad.

Moscow Mule

1 lime

2 oz. vodka

Ginger beer

. . .

Cut lime in half and
squeeze the juice into a
highball glass. Add the spent
lime husks, then top up
the glass with ice. Add vodka,
top up with ginger beer,
stir and serve with a straw.

Hollywood, 1946: frustrated entrepreneur John G. Martin sits in Sunset Boulevard's Cock 'n' Bull Pub, commiserating with its owner. For seven years Martin has been aiming to redeem his dubious acquisition of the assets of the tiny Smirnoff vodka distillery. In those days, "white whiskey" was a mystery to the general drinking public, being the province of a few Slavic émigrés. Meantime, the Cock 'n' Bull's owner was foundering in his attempts to sell homemade ginger beer. Enter an American truism: get two necessities together and they'll mother an invention. The Moscow Mule mixed the vodka and ginger beer into a Cold War highball—and quickly insinuated itself as a drink with movie-star cachet.

MIXING TIPS: Great to serve at parties because of its simplicity. Premix the vodka and lime juices; add the ice and ginger beer as you serve the drinks (don't premix the pop or it will go flat). Don't substitute ginger ale unless you absolutely must; the drink lacks pep without it.

I've travelled a lot in Southeast Asia over the past twenty years, and I find that making this soup always brings back many memories for me. The beautiful flavours such as galangal, lemon grass and kaffir lime leaves are traditional in the cuisines of Indonesia, Malaysia and Thailand. I think that these flavours work well on the west coast because, like those countries, we have an abundance of different seafood. That is what I love about this soup—it is so versatile. It tastes delicious with a number of different types of seafood, which allows you to experiment and use what is available. *Serves 4*

3 Tbsp. olive oil
1 cup chopped galangal
1 cup chopped lemon grass
½ cup chopped kaffir lime leaves
¼ cup peeled and chopped ginger
8 red Thai chiles, finely chopped
5 cloves garlic, peeled and crushed
½ cup chopped onions
½ cup chopped celery
1 cup chopped carrots
8 cups cold water
¼ cup cilantro stems
¼ cup Thai basil stems
1 cup palm sugar (Asian food stores)
¾ cup fish sauce
¾ cup fresh lime juice

4 pieces halibut (each 2 oz.), cleaned
   and skinned
4 oz. mussels, precooked, meat only
4 oz. clams, precooked, meat only
Canned coconut milk to taste
Fresh lime juice to taste
4 scallops, cut horizontally, ⅛-inch
   thick rounds
¼ cup julienned Thai basil leaves
¼ cup cilantro leaves
¼ cup tomato concassé (page 124)
¼ cup snow peas, blanched and
   thinly sliced
¼ cup pea shoots (Asian food stores)
8 tsp. cilantro oil (page 125) for garnish

TO MAKE: Heat olive oil in a stockpot on medium-high heat. Add galangal, lemon grass, kaffir lime leaves, ginger, chiles, garlic, onions, celery and carrots. Sauté for 10 minutes, or until onions are soft and translucent (it is done when you breathe in the aroma and can feel the slight burning sensation of the chile at the back of your throat). Add water, cilantro stems, Thai basil stems, palm sugar, fish sauce and lime juice. Bring to a boil, then remove from the heat and strain through a fine-mesh sieve; discard solids and reserve the broth.

continued overleaf >

TO ASSEMBLE: Reheat the broth in a clean saucepan on medium heat. Add halibut and poach for 1 to 2 minutes. Add mussels and clams. Add coconut milk to taste (first shake the can well to emulsify the milk so that it does not separate). Decrease the heat to medium-low and bring the soup to a gentle simmer (do not allow to boil). Season to taste with salt and a little more lime juice.

Remove halibut from the soup and place a piece in the centre of each of four warmed soup bowls. Scatter thinly sliced scallops, Thai basil, cilantro, tomato concassé, snow peas and pea shoots around halibut in each serving. Remove mussel and clam meat from the soup and divide evenly among the four bowls. Ladle hot soup over ingredients in each bowl. Drizzle 2 teaspoons of cilantro oil around each piece of halibut.

CHICKEN *Noodle* SOUP
WITH *Garlic* CROUTONS

I don't think there was a week that went by, especially in the fall or winter, that I didn't ask my mother to make chicken noodle soup. Truly, this is one of those dishes that you love to have on a cold rainy day. I cannot think of a better soup to make for yourself when you are in need of those comforts of home. *Serves 4*

SOUP
4 half breasts of free-range chicken, boneless, skin on
2 Tbsp. vegetable oil
12 cups dark chicken stock (page 120)
2 cups ¼-inch dice celery
1 cup ¼-inch dice carrots
½ cup 1-inch rounds, baby leeks, white and light green parts only
½ cup peeled and halved pearl onions
½ cup peeled and cooked ¼-inch dice Yukon Gold potatoes
8 oz. dried noodles cooked al dente (makes 4 cups cooked)

CROUTONS
1 baguette
½ cup unsalted butter, softened
1 Tbsp. minced garlic
1 Tbsp. chopped fresh Italian (flat-leaf) parsley
1 Tbsp. chopped fresh chives
¼ cup freshly grated Parmigiano-Reggiano (Parmesan cheese)

TO MAKE SOUP: Preheat the oven to 375°F.

Season outside of chicken breasts with salt and freshly ground white pepper. Heat vegetable oil in an ovenproof frying pan on medium-high heat. Place chicken breasts, skin side down, in frying pan and sear until skin is light golden brown. Turn breasts over and place the pan in the oven. Roast for 10 to 15 minutes, or until desired doneness. Allow to rest for 5 minutes before thinly slicing.

Place dark chicken stock in a saucepan on high heat and boil until reduced by half. Add celery, carrots, leeks and pearl onions. Simmer gently for 5 to 7 minutes, or until vegetables are fork-tender. Add potatoes and noodles, then simmer for another 3 minutes, or until potatoes are warmed through. Season to taste with salt and freshly ground white pepper. Keep warm.

CROUTONS: Preheat the oven to 375°F.

Cut baguette on an angle into four slices that are 1 inch thick. Mix together butter, garlic, parsley and chives in a food processor. Spread herb butter evenly on both sides of baguette slices. Top one side of bread with grated Parmigiano-Reggiano. Place on a baking sheet and toast in the oven for about 10 minutes, or until golden brown.

TO ASSEMBLE: Ladle 1 to 1½ cups of soup into each of four warmed soup bowls. Arrange thinly sliced chicken meat in the centre of each bowl and place a garlic crouton beside it.

SHIITAKE MUSHROOM *Cappuccino*

I grew up with Japanese neighbours who introduced me to a lot of Japanese ingredients, shiitake mushrooms being one of many. I particularly remember having a miso soup with both fresh and dried thinly sliced shiitake mushrooms. This is what gave me the idea to use shiitakes as the main ingredient for a mushroom soup. We present the soup in a cappuccino cup with garlic froth and a sprinkling of dried mushroom powder, hence the name. *Serves 4*

SOUP

1 lb. shiitake mushrooms

¼ cup olive oil

4 Tbsp. sesame oil

2 Tbsp. unsalted butter

½ cup minced onion

2 cloves garlic, peeled and crushed

½ bay leaf

3 sprigs fresh thyme

½ tsp. grated fresh ginger

3 cups mushroom stock (page 121)

1 cup heavy cream

FROTH

1 Tbsp. olive oil

10 to 12 cloves garlic, peeled

1½ tsp. honey

½ cup chicken stock (page 120)

1 cup heavy cream

1 Tbsp. unsalted butter

Powdered porcini for garnish

TO MAKE SOUP: Preheat the grill to medium-high heat.

Remove stems from shiitakes. Chop stems roughly and set aside.

In a stainless steel bowl, toss mushroom caps with olive oil and sesame oil until well coated. Grill for about 4 minutes on each side.

Melt butter in a saucepan on medium heat. Sauté onion and reserved mushroom stems with garlic, bay leaf, thyme and ginger. Add mushroom stock and bring to a boil. Add grilled shiitakes, then decrease the heat to medium-low and simmer for about 10 minutes. Pour in cream and simmer for another 5 to 10 minutes. Remove and discard bay leaf and thyme. Allow mixture to cool for 15 minutes. Purée in a blender or food processor, then strain through a fine-mesh sieve.

TO MAKE FROTH: Heat olive oil in a saucepan on medium heat. Gently sauté garlic for about 4 minutes, or until golden brown. Add honey and cook for about 5 minutes, or until garlic is caramelized, being careful not to burn it. Add chicken stock and simmer for about 10 minutes, or until it is reduced and garlic is glazed and soft. Add ½ cup of the cream and bring to a boil. Decrease the heat to low and simmer for about 5 minutes. Remove from the heat and allow to cool for 15 minutes. Purée in a blender or a food processor, then strain through a fine-mesh sieve.

In another saucepan on medium heat, bring the remaining cream just to a boil. Add garlic purée and season with a little salt. Stir in butter. Keep warm.

TO ASSEMBLE: Reheat soup and season to taste with salt and freshly ground white pepper. You may have to add more stock if the soup is too thick. Ladle soup into four cappuccino cups until three quarters full.

Use a hand-held blender to foam garlic cream sauce until it is frothy. Spoon garlic froth over soup and sprinkle with a little porcini powder.

Negroni

1 oz. gin

1 oz. Campari

1 oz. Italian (red) vermouth

Slice of orange, for garnish

. . .

Pour gin, Campari and
vermouth into a shaker
full of cracked ice and shake
well. Strain into a chilled
cocktail glass. Garnish with
an orange wheel.

Campari, the quintessential Italian aperitif, is the brainchild of Gaspare Campari, one-time master mixologist at Turin's Bass Bar. In the 1850s, at the tender age of fourteen, Gaspare formulated his secret blend of orange rind, spices, tree bark and cochineal (crushed bugs!). His bitter liqueur has inspired dozens of different "campari-nettes"—herbaceous cocktails built from the brilliant red bitter. The Negroni, the foremost of these formulations, is most likely named after Florentine aristocrat Camillo Negroni, who is said to have pioneered the recipe in the 1920s. The initial rush of sweetness from the vermouth is quickly attacked by the bitter finish of the Campari, leaving your palate pleasantly stung and your appetite whetted.

MIXING TIPS: On summer afternoons, serve it as a tall drink, the way Camillo himself originally enjoyed it. Mix the liquors over ice in a highball glass and top up with soda water. Make it this way and leave out the gin, and you've got an Ameri-cano, another of the classic camparinettes.

THE *Beef Dip* WITH HAND-CUT FRIES
AND A *Micro* GREEN SALAD

I wanted to play with what we think of as a traditional sort of British beef dip sandwich—slices of roast beef in a baguette—and make it a little more interesting. Since braised short ribs are on the list of my favourite things to eat, they immediately came to mind. Because the beef is braised, it is very tender and moist. With the addition of juicy caramelized onions, Emmental cheese and a richly flavoured jus, this sandwich is anything but traditional. Of course, any sandwich would not be complete without a few fries on the side, and also a small salad . . . just to ease the guilt. *Serves 4*

BRAISED SHORT RIBS
2 lbs. short ribs, 1¾-inch lengths
2 Tbsp. vegetable oil
3 shallots, peeled and finely chopped
6 cloves garlic, peeled and crushed
1 cup ruby port
1 cup dry red wine
6 cups veal (page 122) or beef stock
   (page 123)
8 sprigs fresh thyme
2 bay leaves

DIPPING SAUCE
1 cup short-rib jus (reduced from short-rib
   cooking liquid)
1 cup veal reduction (page 123)

FRIES
Peanut oil for deep-frying
6 large russet potatoes
Coarse sea salt

SANDWICHES
8 slices sourdough bread, ¾-inch thick
1 cup caramelized onions (page 69)
4 slices Emmental cheese
4 Tbsp. Dijon mustard

SALAD
4 cups micro greens or mesclun
House vinaigrette (page 16)

TO MAKE SHORT RIBS: Preheat the oven to 350°F.

Trim off and discard excess fat from short ribs. Sprinkle both sides with salt and freshly ground white pepper.

Heat vegetable oil in a Dutch oven on medium-high heat. Sear ribs for 5 to 7 minutes, or until brown on all sides. Transfer to a plate and set aside. Pour off all but 1 tablespoon fat from the pan and decrease the heat to medium. Add shallots and garlic, then cook for 2 minutes. Add port and wine, stirring to deglaze the bottom of the pan. Add stock, thyme, bay leaves and browned short ribs, then bring to a boil.

Cover the Dutch oven with aluminum foil, shiny side in, and use a knife to pierce five to six holes in it to allow steam to escape.

continued on page 33 >

Place the Dutch oven in the oven and bake, turning meat occasionally, for 4 to 5 hours, or until meat is falling off the bone. Remove from the oven and allow short ribs to cool in liquid for 1 hour. Take meat off bones. Discard bones and keep meat warm. Reserve cooking liquid to make short-rib jus.

DIPPING SAUCE: Strain cooking liquid from ribs through a fine-mesh sieve into a large saucepan. Bring to a simmer on medium heat and cook for 10 to 12 minutes, or until reduced by half. You should have about 2 cups of rib jus; use 1 cup and set aside the rest for another use. Season rib jus to taste with salt. Add veal reduction and continue cooking for about 10 minutes. Keep warm.

FRIES: Preheat peanut oil for deep-frying to 350°F.

Peel potatoes and cut lengthwise into slices ½ inch thick. Cut each slice into sticks ½ inch wide. Soak in cold water for 10 minutes.

Drain potatoes and dry thoroughly. Blanch potatoes in oil for about 2 minutes, or until softened but not brown. Remove from the oil and drain on a paper towel. Increase temperature of oil to 385°F, then cook potatoes for a second time for about

5 minutes, or until crispy and golden brown. Remove from the oil and drain on a paper towel. Sprinkle with coarse sea salt.

TO ASSEMBLE: Preheat the oven to 375°F.

Toast sourdough slices and place four of them on a baking sheet. Divide caramelized onions among the four slices of toast and top with a piece of cheese. Heat in the oven for 2 to 4 minutes, or until onions are warmed through and cheese melts.

While toast is in the oven, cut short-rib meat into 1-inch pieces and warm with ½ cup of the dipping sauce in a frying pan on medium-high heat until meat is glazed and warmed through. Season to taste with salt and freshly ground white pepper. Spread remaining four slices of toast with Dijon mustard. Divide warmed meat among the toast slices topped with onion and melted cheese, then top with the other slices of toast, mustard-covered side down.

Toss micro greens (or mesclun) in a bowl with house vinaigrette to taste.

Place a sandwich on each of four large plates. Divide fries into four portions and arrange beside sandwiches. Divide salad among plates. Serve warm dipping sauce in individual bowls on the side.

Calamari SANDWICH >

I was in San Diego at a place near the end of the pier called Point Loma Seafoods, where I was introduced to a calamari sandwich. Years later, when I was thinking up ideas for sandwiches for the TV show, I remembered that experience and decided to try making one of my own. You can eat the calamari with the tartar sauce instead of making a sandwich, but the toasted sourdough and sliced tomatoes add a lot. *Serves 4*

TARTAR SAUCE
1 cup mayonnaise (page 127)
3 shiso leaves, roughly chopped (Japanese
    food stores)
¼ cup roughly chopped gherkins
3 Tbsp. capers, rinsed
2 Tbsp. chopped fresh dill
2 Tbsp. chopped fresh tarragon
2 Tbsp. chopped fresh chervil
1 Tbsp. rice vinegar
½ tsp. Dijon mustard

CALAMARI
2 tsp. ground cumin
½ jalapeno, deseeded
2 slices fresh ginger, peeled, ¼-inch thick
2 tsp. curry powder
2 cloves garlic, peeled and roughly
    chopped
16 squid tubes, cleaned, ½-inch rounds
Peanut oil for deep-frying
Tempura batter (page 128)

SANDWICH
8 slices sourdough, 1-inch thick
¼ cup unsalted butter
3 tomatoes, thinly sliced

TO MAKE TARTAR SAUCE: Mix together all tartar sauce ingredients in a bowl. Cover and refrigerate until needed.

CALAMARI: Grind together ground cumin, jalapeno, ginger and curry powder in a food processor or with a mortar and pestle. Transfer the spice mixture to a large bowl and add garlic. Add squid and toss to coat evenly. Season with a little salt and freshly ground white pepper. Cover and marinate for 1 hour in the refrigerator.

Preheat peanut oil for deep-frying to 375°F.

Just before you plan to deep-fry, make the tempura batter. Remove calamari from marinade and coat evenly with tempura batter. Carefully place battered squid, in small batches, in peanut oil and deep-fry for about 3 minutes, or until tempura batter is crisp and light golden brown. Remove calamari from the oil and drain on paper towels. Season lightly with salt. Keep warm.

TO ASSEMBLE: Toast bread, lightly butter each slice and spread on tartar sauce to taste. Place tomato on four slices of toast and season with salt and freshly ground black pepper. Divide calamari among sandwiches and top with a second slice of toasted bread.

PEKING DUCK *Clubhouse*

When Marnie and I were in New York preparing for a James Beard House dinner, a group of us went to a late-night restaurant called Blue Ribbon. Someone gave us a list of things we had to try, and the Peking duck clubhouse was one of them. It was so good that a second visit was required. Years later, we decided to make our own rendition of this clubhouse. It is delicious and messy, the way I think a good sandwich should be. When I prepare this at home, I make sure that I have a few extra napkins on hand. *Serves 4*

8 slices prosciutto

2 half breasts of Peking duck, skin scored and excess fat trimmed

2 Tbsp. vegetable oil

⅓ cup soy sauce

¼ cup sweet sherry

2 Tbsp. oyster sauce

2 Tbsp. brown sugar

¼ tsp. Chinese allspice

2 half breasts of free-range chicken, boneless

12 thin slices fruit and nut bread

Unsalted butter for toast

¼ cup mayonnaise (page 127)

1 half Chinese barbecued duck breast, skin removed, sliced (Asian food stores)

4 leaves lettuce

TO MAKE: Preheat the oven to 375°F.

Place prosciutto on a parchment-lined baking sheet. Bake in the oven for 5 to 7 minutes until crisp. Remove prosciutto from oven to cool but leave the oven on.

Season outside of duck breasts with salt and freshly ground white pepper. Heat 1 tablespoon of the vegetable oil in an ovenproof frying pan on medium-high heat. Sear duck breasts on both sides, for about 1 minute per side. Remove duck from the pan and drain off excess fat.

To the drained frying pan, add soy sauce, sherry, oyster sauce, brown sugar and Chinese allspice. Boil for 4 minutes, then add duck breasts. Continue to cook for about 2 minutes, or until duck is glazed.

Roast in the oven for about 10 minutes for medium-rare, or until desired doneness (longer for more well done, less time for rare). Remove from the oven and allow to rest for 5 minutes before slicing thinly. Reserve duck glaze.

Season outside of chicken breasts with salt and freshly ground white pepper. Heat the remaining vegetable oil in an ovenproof frying pan on medium-high heat. Sear chicken breasts, skin side down, until skin is golden brown. Turn breasts over and place the pan in the oven. Roast for 20 to 25 minutes, or until desired doneness. Remove from the oven and allow to rest for 5 minutes before slicing thinly. Leave the oven on.

TO ASSEMBLE: Place slices of fruit and nut bread on a parchment-lined baking sheet. Lightly toast in the oven or in a toaster. Butter one side of each slice.

Combine mayonnaise and a few tablespoons of duck glaze. Spread a little of the spiced mayonnaise on four of the toast slices, then top each with two slices of crispy prosciutto. Add thinly sliced chicken breast and top with a second slice of toasted bread. Spread with a little more mayonnaise and top with thinly sliced duck breast and a slice of Chinese barbequed duck. Spoon a little duck glaze on top and add a lettuce leaf. Top with a third slice of bread, buttered side down.

Squash and Mascarpone Ravioli
with Truffle Butter / 40

Lumière's Four-Cheese Macaroni / 44

Tripolini Bolognese / 46

Pappardelle with Short-rib Meat,
Toasted Pine Nuts, Tomatoes and Arugula / 49

Caramelized Endive, Blue Cheese
and Walnut Risotto / 52

Lemon-Mint Risotto with
Seared Scallop and Prawns / 54

Pasta & Risotto

SQUASH AND *Mascarpone* RAVIOLI
WITH *Truffle* BUTTER >

*T*his is the most popular dish I've created. It came about because I love squash and I love soft-textured ravioli. Italian recipes usually add bread crumbs to bind the filling, but we cook the squash and let it dry out, so we don't need that. As a result, the filling is soft and the flavour is intense. The handy thing about this recipe is that the ravioli can be made in advance and kept frozen. Between the rich egg pasta dough, the roasted squash and mascarpone filling, and the truffle butter sauce, every mouthful is decadent. *Serves 4*

FILLING

2 butternut squash (each 1½ lbs.), halved and deseeded
Olive oil
4 Tbsp. mascarpone
½ tsp. ground nutmeg
2 Tbsp. freshly grated Parmigiano-
  Reggiano (Parmesan cheese)

RAVIOLI (page 129)

SAUCE

¼ cup rice vinegar
¼ cup dry white wine
1 tsp. heavy cream, optional
¼ to ½ cup unsalted butter, ½-inch
  cubes, chilled
1 Tbsp. fresh lemon juice
¼ tsp. white truffle oil
2 Tbsp. finely chopped black truffle or
  ¼ tsp. white truffle oil

Fleur de sel for garnish

TO MAKE FILLING: Preheat the oven to 325°F.

Coat the cut sides of squash with a little olive oil, then season with salt and freshly ground white pepper. Place cut side down on a parchment-lined baking sheet. Bake in the oven for 20 to 30 minutes, or until cooked through and soft. Remove from the oven and allow to cool. Scoop out flesh. Reserve 2 cups of squash for the recipe. (Freeze the rest for use in another recipe; will keep in the freezer for up to 6 months.)

Purée squash, mascarpone and nutmeg in a blender or food processor until very smooth. Press mixture through a fine-mesh sieve, using the back of a wooden spoon or a spatula to remove any lumps. Add Parmigiano-Reggiano. Season to taste with salt and freshly ground white pepper. Cover and refrigerate until ready to use.

RAVIOLI: Make ravioli recipe and fill with squash filling.

SAUCE: Combine rice vinegar and wine in a saucepan on medium heat, then reduce until the liquid forms a light syrup. (If you are not experienced at making butter sauces, you can prevent the sauce from splitting by adding the optional cream.) Decrease the heat to low and whisk in butter, one piece at a time, until well incorporated. Do not boil. Add lemon juice, truffle oil and truffle (or an addi-

tional ¼ teaspoon truffle oil). Season to taste with salt. Set aside and keep warm. When reheating, be careful not to boil the sauce as it may split.

TO ASSEMBLE: Bring a large saucepan with 6 quarts of salted water to a boil. Add ravioli in small batches and cook for 3 to 4 minutes, or until pasta is al dente. Drain.

(Ravioli can be cooked ahead of time and reheated by dipping into boiling water for 20 to 30 seconds.)

Place 5 to 10 ravioli on each of four warmed plates. Spoon warmed truffle sauce over ravioli and sprinkle with a little fleur de sel.

Papa Doble

When Ernest Hemingway settled in Cuba during WWII, he brought his Underwood typewriter, his fishing boat and his insatiable thirst with him. The day he strode into Havana's Floridita Bar and met Constante Ribailagua marked the collision of one of history's celebrated imbibers with one of Cocktaildom's master bar-men. Papa developed such a predilection for the mixing maestro's "Daiquiri No. 3" and its accent of fresh grapefruit juice that it soon became his trademark drink. Modified to be mixed with a double measure of rum and no sugar, it become a Papa Doble ("papa's double").

MIXING TIPS: This particular recipe comes from A.E. Hotchner, Papa's unofficial biographer. The Papa Doble is a tart, sugarless drink by design—resist the urge to sweeten it up. Maraschino liqueur has nothing to do with the unnaturally red cherries you see garnishing Shirley Temples (and *for shame*, Manhattans) but is a semi-dry liqueur made in Italy, from marasca cherries and their pits. You can mix an acceptable substitute from 4 parts Kirschwasser and 1 part simple syrup for cocktails (page 126).

3 oz. white rum

¾ oz. fresh lime juice

¾ oz. fresh pink grapefruit juice

¼ oz. maraschino liqueur

Wedge of lime

. . .

Pour rum, lime juice, grapefruit juice and maraschino liqueur into a shaker full of cracked ice and shake well. Strain into a chilled cocktail glass. Rub a lime wedge around the rim.

*O*riginally, Marnie and I created a version of this for the TV show, *New Classics.* My kitchen staff gave this recipe a little facelift and made it into the great dish that it is today. It is a very rich dish and can take away any feeling of hunger in just a few mouthfuls. An upscale comfort food. *Serves 4*

BÉCHAMEL SAUCE

4 cups milk

2 cloves garlic, peeled and crushed

4 Tbsp. unsalted butter

4 Tbsp. all-purpose flour

Pinch of freshly grated nutmeg

MACARONI AND CHEESE

2 tsp. vegetable oil

8 oz. Irish or double-smoked bacon, finely diced

4 shallots, peeled and finely chopped

¼ cup grated Emmental

¼ cup crumbled blue cheese

¼ cup grated sharp white Cheddar

½ cup freshly grated Pecorino Romano

12 oz. dried succhietto pasta, cooked al dente

TO MAKE BÉCHAMEL SAUCE: Combine milk and garlic in a saucepan on medium heat. Bring to a boil and remove from the heat. Cover and leave to infuse for 10 minutes. Strain through a fine-mesh strainer and discard solids.

Make a roux by melting butter in a heavy-bottomed saucepan on medium heat. Whisk in flour and cook for about 1 minute, or until light brown. Remove from the heat and allow to cool slightly. Add strained hot milk, whisking constantly.

Return the saucepan to medium heat and bring the mixture back to a boil, whisking constantly until sauce thickens. Add nutmeg, then season to taste with salt and freshly ground white pepper. Allow to simmer for a further 3 minutes. Remove from the heat.

TO ASSEMBLE: Preheat the oven to 375°F.

Heat vegetable oil in a frying pan on medium heat. Sauté bacon and shallots for about 5 minutes, or until bacon is just cooked and shallots are translucent.

Reheat béchamel sauce on medium-low heat and whisk in Emmental, blue cheese, Cheddar and half of the Pecorino Romano. Add half of the bacon-shallot mixture.

Divide cooked pasta into four individual 3-cup casserole dishes and pour sauce over (enough to cover pasta by ½ inch). Sprinkle the tops with the remaining Pecorino Romano and the remaining bacon-shallot mixture. Bake in the oven for 10 to 15 minutes, or until hot and bubbling. Place under the broiler for 3 to 5 minutes, or until top is light golden brown.

Place each casserole dish on a napkin-lined plate.

TRIPOLINI *Bolognese*

When I crave comfort food, I make tripolini Bolognese. This particular meat sauce is a combination of the classic Italian version that uses beef and vegetables, and the French version that uses lean pork. Best of all, this sauce can be made in a large batch and frozen, for when that craving hits you. *Serves 4*

1 medium carrot, peeled
1 stalk celery, washed
½ onion, peeled
1 large clove garlic, peeled
¼ cup chopped fresh sage leaves
2 Tbsp. chopped fresh rosemary leaves
2 Tbsp. fresh thyme leaves
5 Tbsp. olive oil
8 oz. ground veal
8 oz. ground pork
¼ cup finely diced pancetta
¼ cup dry white wine
¼ cup tomato paste
1½ cups veal stock (page 122)
4½ cups chicken stock (page 120)
½ cup heavy cream
1 lb. dried tripolini pasta, cooked al dente
¼ cup freshly grated Parmigiano-Reggiano
  (Parmesan cheese)
2 Tbsp. unsalted butter
2 Tbsp. extra-virgin olive oil
Freshly grated Parmigiano-Reggiano for
  garnish

TO MAKE: Combine carrot, celery, onion, garlic, sage, rosemary and thyme in a food processor. Process until finely minced.

Heat olive oil in a large heavy-bottomed frying pan on medium-high heat. Add ground veal and pork. Season to taste with salt and freshly ground white pepper. Cook until meat is well browned, using a wooden spoon to break up lumps. Remove meat from the pan and drain through a sieve. Reserve meat and discard fat. Reserve the pan.

In a large saucepan, sauté pancetta on medium heat until crispy. Add minced vegetable-herb mixture. Sauté on medium-low heat for about 10 minutes, or until vegetables are soft and translucent. Add cooked ground meat. Add wine and continue to cook until liquid is reduced by half. Add tomato paste, veal stock and 2½ cups of the chicken stock. Increase the heat to medium and continue to cook until the liquid is reduced again by half. Season to taste with salt and freshly ground white pepper. (The Bolognese sauce can be made ahead up to this point and stored in airtight containers; will keep in the refrigerator for up to 1 week or in the freezer for up to 6 months.)

Combine Bolognese sauce and the remaining chicken stock in a large saucepan. Cook on medium heat for 8 to 10 minutes, or until reduced by half. Stir in cream. Add cooked pasta, Parmigiano-Reggiano, butter and extra-virgin olive oil. Toss to combine well and reheat thoroughly. Season to taste with salt and freshly ground white pepper.

TO ASSEMBLE: Divide pasta among four large warmed pasta bowls. Garnish with a sprinkling of freshly grated Parmigiano-Reggiano.

PAPPARDELLE WITH *Short-rib* MEAT, TOASTED PINE NUTS, *Tomatoes* AND ARUGULA

Short ribs are the key element in this dish. We have incorporated arugula, which adds a slightly bitter freshness to the sauce and helps to balance the richness of the short ribs, as well as pine nuts, which add texture. *Serves 4*

1 Tbsp. olive oil

2 tsp. minced chiles

1 Tbsp. minced garlic

2 cups short-rib jus (page 31)

2 cups short-rib meat (page 31)

2 cups tomato sauce (page 124)

1 lb. dried pappardelle, cooked al dente

4 cups arugula

1 cup freshly grated Parmigiano-Reggiano
    (Parmesan cheese)

¼ cup extra-virgin olive oil

½ cup toasted pine nuts

TO MAKE: Heat olive oil in a frying pan on medium-high heat. Sauté minced chiles and garlic for 20 to 30 seconds, or until almost golden. Add short-rib jus, short-rib meat and tomato sauce. Season with salt and freshly ground white pepper. Cook until sauce is reduced by half. Add cooked pappardelle, arugula and Parmigiano-Reggiano. Toss to coat pasta evenly. Finish with extra-virgin olive oil and toss to coat thoroughly.

TO ASSEMBLE: Use tongs to divide pasta among four warmed pasta bowls. Pour any sauce that remains in the saucepan onto pasta. Sprinkle with toasted pine nuts.

Scotch and Lime

1 whole lime, washed
and quartered
1 tsp. simple syrup
for cocktails (page 126)
2 oz. blended Scotch

. . .

Squeeze juice from
lime quarters into a chilled
rocks glass and add
the lime husks. Add simple
syrup and Scotch. Muddle
all ingredients together.
If you don't have a muddler,
use the handle of a wooden
spoon. Top with ice and
stir. Serve with a stir stick.

This sour is a newfound favourite and main-stay of our afterwork ablutions. The unlikely but balanced blend of malted barley sweetness and cutting citrus provides a surprising, smoky delight. Although similar in ingredients to other sours, the unique mixing procedure, borrowed from the popular South American Caipirinha, makes this pulpy ice-peaked tumbler unique.

MIXING TIPS: Use a blended Scotch and don't waste your single malt. Instead of Scotch, you can use cachaça to make the Brazilian Caipirinha; or white rum for a Caipirissima, or vodka for a Caipiroska.

Muddle the limes thoroughly to release the oils from the peel. This adds a nice complexity to the drink's flavour.

CARAMELIZED *Endive*, BLUE CHEESE AND *Walnut* RISOTTO

Among the foods that I consider to be comforting is risotto. It is a dish that can be eaten at lunch or dinner. The creamy texture of the risotto, the saltiness of the blue cheese and the crunch of the walnuts, along with the slightly bitter radicchio and the sweet, braised endive, offer a perfect combination to tease your palate. *Serves 4*

ENDIVE

4 large Belgian endives
2 Tbsp. grapeseed oil
3 tsp. granulated sugar
⅓ cup vegetable stock (page 121)

RISOTTO

3 to 4 cups vegetable stock
6 Tbsp. olive oil
4 large shallots, peeled and finely
   chopped
2 cups arborio or carnaroli rice,
   superfino quality
2 cups dry white wine
¼ cup thinly sliced radicchio
2 to 4 Tbsp. freshly grated Parmigiano-
   Reggiano (Parmesan cheese)
4 Tbsp. unsalted butter
4 Tbsp. mascarpone
½ cup Roquefort cheese, crumbled
¼ cup walnut pieces, toasted

TO MAKE ENDIVE: Cut each endive in half lengthwise; remove and discard the cores. Heat grapeseed oil in a large non-stick frying pan on medium-high heat. Sear endives on both sides until light brown. Sprinkle them with sugar and cook for 3 to 5 minutes, or until golden and caramelized.

Decrease the heat to medium-low, add stock and cover the pan with a lid. Cook for 10 to 12 minutes, or until endive is fork-tender. Remove from the heat and allow to cool. Endives can be cut in half again for serving or left as is.

RISOTTO: Place stock in a saucepan on medium heat and bring to a gentle simmer. Keep hot.

In another saucepan, heat olive oil on medium heat. Sauté shallots until translucent (do not brown). Add rice and cook for 3 to 5 minutes, stirring so grains are well coated with oil. Add wine, stir gently and cook until liquid is absorbed.

Add ½ cup of hot stock at a time, bring to a simmer and stir gently; wait until each addition is nearly all absorbed before adding more. Do not stir too often or too hard, as you risk breaking the grains. Continue this process until the risotto has cooked for about 15 minutes. At this point, the risotto should be al dente (firm and tender), moist and almost creamy.

To finish risotto, gently stir in radicchio, Parmigiano-Reggiano, butter and mascarpone. Season to taste with salt and freshly ground white pepper.

TO ASSEMBLE: Divide risotto among four warmed pasta bowls, about 1 to 1½ cups per serving. Place endives on a plate and reheat in a microwave on high for 45 seconds. Lay a portion of endive to the side of the risotto on each plate. Top risotto with crumbled Roquefort cheese and toasted walnuts.

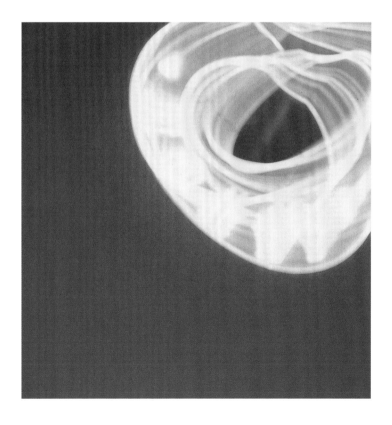

LEMON-MINT *Risotto* WITH SEARED SCALLOP AND *Prawns* >

*M*arnie Coldham, one of my sous chefs and co-author, knows that I love risotto, so she came up with this idea and approached me with it. I liked it so much that we put it on the menu the following day, and it has been there ever since. Seafood risotto is wonderful on its own, but the additions of mint and lemon zest take it a step beyond. *Serves 4*

RISOTTO

3 to 4 cups chicken stock (page 120)

6 Tbsp. olive oil

4 large shallots, peeled and finely chopped

2 cups arborio or carnaroli rice, superfino quality

2 cups dry white wine

2 to 4 Tbsp. freshly grated Parmigiano-Reggiano (Parmesan cheese)

4 Tbsp. unsalted butter

4 Tbsp. mascarpone

½ cup ¼-inch dice preserved lemons (page 126)

4 Tbsp. lemon zest

3 Tbsp. julienned fresh mint leaves

SCALLOP AND PRAWNS

4 large scallops

8 Tbsp. olive oil

12 prawns, shelled and deveined

2 Tbsp. unsalted butter

Mint oil (page 125) for garnish
Chervil for garnish

TO MAKE RISOTTO: Place stock in a saucepan on medium heat and bring to a gentle simmer. Keep hot.

In another saucepan, heat olive oil on medium heat. Sauté shallots until translucent (do not brown). Add rice and cook for 3 to 5 minutes, stirring so grains are well coated with oil. Add wine, stir gently and cook until liquid is absorbed.

Add ½ cup of hot stock at a time, bring to a simmer and stir gently; wait until each addition is nearly all absorbed before adding more. Do not stir too often or too hard, as you risk breaking the grains. Continue this process until the risotto has cooked for about 15 minutes. At this point, the risotto should be al dente (firm and tender), moist and almost creamy.

Gently fold in Parmigiano-Reggiano, butter, mascarpone, preserved lemons, lemon zest and mint. Season to taste with salt and freshly ground white pepper. Keep warm.

SCALLOP AND PRAWNS: Season scallops on both sides with salt and freshly ground white pepper. Heat 4 tablespoons of the olive oil in a nonstick frying pan on high heat. Sear scallops for 1½ minutes on each side. Remove from the heat and allow to rest for 2 minutes.

Season prawns with salt. In a clean nonstick frying pan, or two pans so as not to crowd prawns, heat the remaining 4 tablespoons olive oil on medium-high heat. Sauté prawns on one side for about 1 minute, or until they turn pink. Add butter, turn prawns over and cook for 1 more minute. Remove from the heat.

TO ASSEMBLE: Divide risotto among four warmed pasta bowls. Place one scallop and three prawns on top of each serving and drizzle a little mint oil around the shellfish. Garnish each scallop with a small sprig of chervil.

Sake and Maple Marinated Sablefish
with Hijiki-Soy Sauce / 58

Pan-seared Black Bass with Preserved
Lemon and Prawn Compote / 63

Sardines Gremolata / 64

Sole, Chanterelle and Spinach
Casserole in White Wine Cream / 65

Roast Chicken with Choucroute
and Pomme Purée / 66

Lumière Shepherd's Pie: Duck Confit,
Caramelized Onions and Truffled
Pomme Purée / 69

Crispy Leg of Duck Confit with
Lentils and Caramelized Apples / 72

Lumière's Cassoulet / 74

Confit of Lamb Shoulder with Ratatouille / 78

Côte de Boeuf with Roasted Portobello
Mushrooms and Bordelaise Sauce / 80

Fish, Poultry & Meat

SAKE AND *Maple* MARINATED SABLEFISH
WITH *Hijiki-Soy* SAUCE

*Y*ears ago, when I was working in Japan, I was inspired to create this dish. I wanted to use sake and combine it with a truly Canadian product. And what better typifies Canada than maple syrup? When baked, this marinade caramelizes and the sweetness matches perfectly with the oily, rich flesh of the sablefish. The saltiness of the hijiki-soy sauce balances out the sweetness of the marinade. (Hijiki is a seaweed that is harvested off the coast of Japan—it grows in thin strands and is delicious.) And there's the added richness of short-rib meat. Try it and you will see why this has become a Lumière signature dish. *Serves 4*

SABLEFISH

1½ cups sake

⅔ cup maple syrup

4 fillets sablefish (each 5 oz.), skin on and scaled

SAUCE

2 Tbsp. hijiki (Asian or Japanese food stores)

1 cup cold water

⅔ cup dark chicken stock (page 120)

½ tsp. minced ginger

⅔ cup heavy cream

1 tsp. light soy sauce or tamari

GARNISH

2 Tbsp. unsalted butter

1 cup peeled and ½-inch dice Yukon Gold potatoes

3 leeks, white and light green parts only, ½-inch thick rounds

1½ to 2 cups dark chicken stock (page 120)

¼ cup shredded short-rib meat, optional (page 31)

TO MAKE SABLEFISH: Bring sake to a boil in a saucepan on high heat, then stir in maple syrup. Remove from the heat and let cool.

Place sablefish fillets in a deep airtight container. Pour sake and maple syrup mixture over fish to cover. Put lid on container and place in the refrigerator to marinate for 24 hours.

SAUCE: Place hijiki in a bowl, add water and set aside.

Combine stock and ginger in a saucepan on medium heat and bring to a boil. Decrease heat to low and simmer for about 5 minutes. Strain through a fine-mesh sieve into a clean saucepan on medium heat. Stir in cream and light soy sauce (or tamari), and bring to a boil. Remove from the heat and set aside.

GARNISH: Melt butter in a large frying pan on medium heat. Sauté potatoes for about 5 minutes, or until three quarters cooked. Add leeks and 1½ cups of the stock. Season to taste with salt and freshly ground white pepper. Continue to cook for another 3 to 5 minutes, or until potatoes are soft (be careful not to overcook or potatoes will lose their shape and fall apart). The stock should be mostly absorbed and glaze the leek and potatoes. Remove from the heat and set aside.

TO FINISH SABLEFISH: Preheat the oven to 375°F.

Take out sablefish from marinade and pat dry. Place fish, skin side up, on a parchment-lined baking sheet. Bake in the oven for 10 to 12 minutes, or until done (the flesh flakes easily).

TO ASSEMBLE: Reheat potato-leek mixture and divide evenly among four large warmed plates.

Heat short-rib meat (optional) with a few tablespoons of stock, then season to taste with salt and freshly ground white pepper. Arrange a quarter of the short-rib meat on top of potato-leek mixture on each plate.

Remove and discard skin from sablefish. Place a piece of fish on top of each serving. Strain rehydrated hijiki through a fine-mesh sieve and discard liquid. Sprinkle 1 teaspoon of hijiki over each portion of fish.

Reheat soy-ginger sauce to a simmer. Use a handheld blender to froth the broth and spoon over fish.

Champagne Cocktail

Sugar cube

2 or 3 dashes angostura bitters

5 oz. Champagne

Lemon twist

. . .

In a flute, saturate a
sugar cube with angostura
bitters. Top up the glass
with Champagne and garnish
with a lemon twist.

This elegant aperitif is the original and most popular of the sparkling wine cocktails. It dates from the 1860s and, apart from a few playful variations, has remained virtually unchanged. The addition of sweet and bitter tones imparts a new and exciting depth to the Champagne's flavour—yielding this great classic.

MIXING TIPS: Splurge on Champagne and use the real thing when making this cocktail—you'll thank yourself.

PAN-SEARED *Black Bass* WITH PRESERVED
LEMON AND *Prawn* COMPOTE

I love to simply pan-fry fish. It reminds me of when I was a kid, trout fishing with my dad and cooking the catch of the day over an open flame. To set off that simplicity, we serve the fish with a savoury prawn compote and a spicy garnish of green beans with anchovy and chili. *Serves 4*

PRAWN COMPOTE

3 Tbsp. extra-virgin olive oil
6 large prawns, peeled and deveined
¼ cup tomato concassé
¼ cup diced preserved lemon (page 126)
2 Tbsp. capers, rinsed
3 tsp. finely chopped fresh tarragon
3 tsp. finely chopped fresh Italian
　(flat-leaf) parsley
½ tsp. sherry vinegar
½ tsp. black olive tapenade (page 10) or
　pitted and finely chopped black olives

BASS

3 Tbsp. olive oil
4 black bass fillets (each 4 oz.), skin on,
　scaled and scored

GARNISH

2 Tbsp. unsalted butter
2 cups fresh thin green beans, blanched
1 anchovy fillet, minced
¼ tsp. sambal oelek (Asian chili paste)
Pinch of minced garlic
¾ cup veal reduction (page 123)
Parsley oil to garnish (page 125)

TO MAKE PRAWN COMPOTE: Heat 1 tablespoon of the olive oil in a frying pan on medium-high heat. Sauté prawns for 1 to 2 minutes, or until they turn pink. Transfer prawns to a plate to cool.

Combine tomato concassé, preserved lemon, capers, tarragon, parsley, sherry vinegar and the remaining olive oil in a bowl. Roughly chop cooled prawns, then add prawns and their juice to tomato mixture. Cover and refrigerate until ready to use.

BASS: Heat olive oil in a large nonstick frying pan on high heat. Season bass with a little salt and freshly ground white pepper. Sauté skin side down for 1 to 2 minutes on each side, or until done (flesh is opaque). Remove fish from the pan and blot off excess oil.

GARNISH: Melt butter in a frying pan on medium heat. Add green beans and reheat for 2 to 3 minutes. Add anchovy, sambal oelek and garlic. Season to taste with salt and freshly ground white pepper.

Place veal reduction in a saucepan on medium heat and bring to a boil. Keep warm.

TO ASSEMBLE: Divide green beans among four warmed plates. Top each serving with a piece of bass, placed skin side up. Stir black olive tapenade (or finely chopped black olives) into chilled prawn compote. Spoon a quarter of the compote onto each serving of fish. Place a couple of tablespoons of veal reduction on each plate and drizzle with a little parsley oil.

Sardines GREMOLATA

*S*ardines are a favourite in Mediterranean countries like Spain and Portugal. Now, they have become readily available and are growing in popularity. The lemon and herbs in the gremolata set off the oiliness of the sardines beautifully. This dish takes no time to prepare. My philosophy about cooking fish has always been to keep the flavours simple. *Serves 4*

GREMOLATA

2 cups panko (Japanese bread crumbs)
2 cups finely grated Parmigiano-Reggiano
    (Parmesan cheese)
1 Tbsp. minced garlic
2 Tbsp. grated lemon zest
2 Tbsp. finely chopped preserved lemon
    (page 126)
2 Tbsp. finely chopped fresh parsley
2 Tbsp. finely chopped fresh chives
½ cup clarified butter (page 127)
2 Tbsp. extra-virgin olive oil

SARDINES

6 sardines, scaled and filleted
4 lemon wedges, deseeded
4 lime wedges, deseeded

TO MAKE GREMOLATA: Combine all gremolata ingredients in a bowl. Mixture should stick together when gently squeezed in your hand. If too dry, add a little more clarified butter. Season to taste with salt and freshly cracked black pepper.

SARDINES: Preheat the oven to 375°F.

Place 3 sardine fillets in the bottom of each of four small shallow casserole serving dishes. Divide gremolata among dishes, placing in a loose layer on top of fish; use your hand to gently pat it down. Bake in the oven for 15 to 20 minutes, or until light golden brown. Remove from the oven.

TO SERVE: Place the casserole dishes on four napkin-lined plates. Arrange lemon and lime wedges on the side.

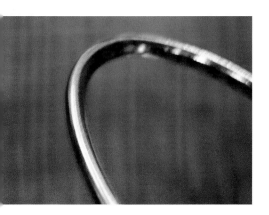

SOLE, CHANTERELLE AND *Spinach* CASSEROLE
IN WHITE *Wine* CREAM

This is a memorable dish for me in many ways. When I was working in Sweden, the family that I lived with often went ice fishing in the winter for flatfish or sole. This is the dish that they used to make with the fish they caught. It's a very simple dish, and one that you can put together quickly when you don't have a lot of time. You can even make it the day before, then just reheat and serve. *Serves 4*

3 cups dark chicken stock (page 120)
1 Tbsp. minced garlic
1 cup heavy cream
2 Tbsp. olive oil
3 Tbsp. unsalted butter
3 cups chanterelles, quartered
3 lbs. sole fillets
1 lemon, juice of
1 large Yukon Gold potato, peeled and thinly sliced
½ onion, peeled and thinly sliced
2 bunches spinach, blanched
¼ cup chopped fresh dill
¼ cup chopped fresh chervil
¼ cup chopped fresh Italian (flat-leaf) parsley
2 Tbsp. chopped fresh tarragon
2 Tbsp. chopped fresh chives
⅓ cup dry white wine

TO MAKE: Preheat the oven to 375°F.

Combine chicken stock and garlic in a saucepan on medium-high heat and simmer for 3 to 5 minutes. Add cream and cook until reduced by one third. Remove from the heat and set aside.

Heat olive oil and 2 tablespoons of the butter in a frying pan on medium-high heat. Sauté chanterelles for about 1 minute. Season with salt and freshly ground white pepper. Add the remaining 1 tablespoon butter and continue to cook mushrooms for 5 to 8 minutes, or until light golden brown.

Grease the inside of a 3-quart casserole dish with a little olive oil. Arrange half of sole in the bottom of the dish to form one layer. Season with salt, freshly ground white pepper and half of the lemon juice. Add potato in one layer, onion in one layer and a layer of the remaining sole. Add spinach in one layer, and add chanterelles in one layer.

Sprinkle with dill, chervil, parsley, tarragon and chives. Ladle reduced stock-cream mixture over top. Top with white wine. Bake casserole in the oven for 60 to 75 minutes, or until done (a knife should pierce easily through all the layers).

TO SERVE: Place the casserole dish on a napkin-lined plate and serve family style.

ROAST *Chicken* WITH CHOUCROUTE
AND *Pomme* PURÉE

The key elements in making choucroute are a very flavourful bacon and
a good Riesling to give it the necessary
acidity. Those are what I think really make
this dish. The choucroute tastes best when
it is made a few days ahead. The tangy
spiced choucroute, the buttery pomme
purée, the sweet sauce and the savoury
roast chicken offer an array of balanced
flavours. *Serves 4*

CHICKEN
2 small young chickens (each 1 to 1½ lbs.)
1 lemon, quartered
8 sprigs fresh thyme
4 cloves garlic, small, crushed
¼ cup unsalted butter, softened

SPICE SACHET
1 star anise
2 whole cloves
½ tsp. mustard seeds
½ tsp. coriander seeds
¼ tsp. white peppercorns
2 juniper berries, crushed
1 bay leaf
½ inch cinnamon stick

CHOUCROUTE
1 Tbsp. unsalted butter
1 Tbsp. rendered duck fat (page 127)
½ cup julienned double-smoked bacon
2 cups peeled and thinly sliced onions
2 cups dry Riesling
1 cup drained sauerkraut

POMME PURÉE
1¼ lbs. Yukon Gold potatoes, skin on
½ cup heavy cream, lukewarm
¼ cup unsalted butter, ½-inch cubes,
   softened

SAUCE
2 cups ice wine or dry Riesling
1 Tbsp. rice vinegar
2 Tbsp. soy sauce
1 Tbsp. grainy mustard
2 Tbsp. unsalted butter
2 tsp. fresh lemon juice

TO MAKE CHICKEN: Preheat the oven
to 375°F.

Season cavities of chickens with salt
and freshly ground white pepper. Place 2
lemon quarters, 4 thyme sprigs and 2 garlic
cloves inside each bird. Truss each with
kitchen string.

Place butter in a bowl and season generously with salt and freshly ground white
pepper. Rub butter mixture over skin of
chickens. Place birds on a platter and
refrigerate for 10 minutes to harden butter.

Place chickens on a rack in a large roasting pan. Roast in the oven, basting
periodically to ensure the skin becomes
nice and brown, for 35 to 45 minutes, or
until the juices run clear.

While chickens are roasting, make the spice sachet, choucroute, pomme purée and sauce.

When chickens are done, take them out of the oven and allow to rest for 10 minutes. Remove and discard the string. Use a sharp knife to cut off each leg with thigh attached. Cut off each half breast in one piece.

SPICE SACHET: Place all sachet ingredients in the centre of a 6-inch square of cheesecloth. Roll up loosely and tie closed with a piece of kitchen string to make a sachet.

CHOUCROUTE: Melt butter and duck fat in a large saucepan on medium heat. Sauté bacon and onions for about 10 minutes, or until bacon is cooked and onions are transparent. Add wine, sauerkraut and spice sachet, and continue to cook until liquid is all absorbed. Remove and discard spice sachet, then season to taste with salt and freshly ground white pepper. Keep warm.

POMME PURÉE: Leave skin on potatoes to prevent them from absorbing excess water, which would make the purée too moist. Place potatoes in a saucepan, add enough salted water to cover and bring to a boil on high heat. Decrease the heat to medium and simmer for 15 to 20 minutes, or until potatoes are fork-tender. Drain.

Peel potatoes and pass through a ricer or a fine-mesh sieve into a clean saucepan on medium-low heat. Slowly fold lukewarm cream into potatoes, then gently fold in butter, one piece at a time. Be careful not to mix the potatoes too quickly or vigorously when adding cream and butter, as mixture will become gluey. Season to taste with salt and freshly ground white pepper.

Press whipped potatoes again through a fine-mesh sieve into a clean saucepan. Cover tightly with plastic wrap, gently pressing it onto the surface of potatoes to prevent drying out or a crust from forming. Keep warm until ready to serve.

SAUCE: Combine ice wine (or dry Riesling), rice vinegar and soy sauce in a saucepan on medium-high heat. Bring to a boil and reduce by one third. Strain through a fine-mesh sieve into another saucepan on medium heat. Stir in grainy mustard and bring to a simmer. Decrease the heat to low and slowly whisk in butter, a bit at a time. Add lemon juice. Season with salt and freshly ground white pepper. Keep warm.

TO ASSEMBLE: Divide choucroute among four warmed dinner plates. Place leg and attached thigh, and a half breast on top of each serving. For each serving, take one quarter of the pomme purée, form it into a quenelle shape and place beside chicken. Pour sauce over and around chicken.

LUMIÈRE *Shepherd's* PIE: DUCK CONFIT, CARAMELIZED *Onions* AND TRUFFLED POMME PURÉE

The chefs in my kitchen frequently make shepherd's pie for the staff meal. I thought it was so good that we should put the dish on the bar menu. We use duck confit on the bottom layer, topped with truffled pomme purée. In between, there are layers of caramelized onion and roasted corn. Instead of making small individual servings, you can make it in a large baking dish. You can even prepare it a day ahead, then simply bake it in the oven and serve. *Serves 6*

CARAMELIZED ONIONS
¼ cup vegetable oil
3 medium onions, peeled and thinly sliced
7 sprigs thyme, tied in a bundle

ROASTED CORN
2 Tbsp. vegetable oil
2 Tbsp. unsalted butter
2 cups fresh corn kernels

POMME PURÉE
1¼ lbs. Yukon Gold potatoes, skin on
1 cup heavy cream, lukewarm
5 Tbsp. unsalted butter
1 tsp. white truffle oil
1 Tbsp. chopped black truffle
Fine sea salt to taste

½ recipe duck confit (page 72)
1 cup veal reduction (page 123)
Fleur de sel for garnish

TO MAKE CARAMELIZED ONIONS: Heat vegetable oil in a large saucepan on medium heat. Sauté onions and thyme until onions are soft and transparent. Increase heat to medium-high and cook, stirring with a wooden spoon and scraping the bottom of the pot to prevent burning, for 8 to 10 minutes, or until onions are caramelized. When onions turn dark brown, remove from the heat. Take out and discard thyme. Season to taste with salt and freshly ground white pepper. Allow onions to cool, then place in an airtight container and refrigerate until needed.

ROASTED CORN: Preheat a large frying pan on medium-high heat. Add vegetable oil and butter. Add corn and cook for 15 to 20 minutes, or until golden brown. Remove from the heat and allow to cool.

POMME PURÉE: Place potatoes, skin on, in a medium saucepan. Cover with cold lightly salted water and bring to a boil on high heat. Decrease heat to medium and simmer for 15 to 20 minutes, or until potatoes are fork-tender. Peel potatoes and pass through a ricer or a fine-mesh sieve.

continued overleaf >

Place riced potatoes in a saucepan on medium-low heat and fold in lukewarm cream, butter and truffle oil. Season to taste with salt. Add truffle.

Cover with plastic wrap, gently pressing it down on the surface of potatoes to prevent drying out or a crust from forming. Keep warm until ready to use.

TO ASSEMBLE: Preheat the oven to 375°F.

Remove and discard the skin from confit duck legs and thighs. Use a fork to shred the meat off the bone, making sure to remove and discard any cartilage or small bones.

Use a little vegetable oil to grease the sides of six metal ring molds or ramekins, 3 inches in diameter and 3 inches high. Place molds or ramekins on a parchment-lined baking sheet. Place equal amounts of shredded duck meat in the bottom of each mold or ramekin. Mix together caramelized onions and caramelized corn in a bowl, then place mixture on top of duck meat, pressing down gently to fit tightly and evenly. Fill molds or ramekins to the top with truffled pomme purée.

Bake in the oven for 5 to 10 minutes, or until thoroughly warmed and the potatoes are golden brown on top. Remove from the oven and allow to rest for 5 minutes.

Heat veal reduction in a saucepan on high heat. Keep warm.

TO SERVE: For shepherd's pies in molds, place each one on a warmed plate and use a small paring knife to cut around the inside and then unmold it. Sprinkle a little fleur de sel on top and spoon veal reduction around edge.

For shepherd's pies in ramekins, do not cut around the inside as they are served in the dishes. Place each ramekin on a napkin-lined plate. Sprinkle a little fleur de sel on top and serve veal reduction in a small pitcher on the side.

CRISPY LEG OF *Duck* CONFIT WITH LENTILS
AND *Caramelized* APPLES

To my way of thinking, no bistro/ brasserie menu is complete unless it offers duck confit. There is a lot to do to make this recipe, but it is easier than it looks, as each component can be made ahead of time. You might want to double the duck confit recipe to use half in this dish and keep half to make the dish again later or for another use. *Serves 4*

DUCK CONFIT
1 clove garlic, peeled and roughly chopped
1 bay leaf
4 sprigs fresh thyme
4 Tbsp. coarse sea salt
1½ tsp. black peppercorns
4 duck legs, thighs attached
3 to 4 cups rendered duck fat (page 127) or lard

LENTILS
1 Tbsp. unsalted butter
1 Tbsp. olive oil
3 strips double-smoked bacon
1 shallot, peeled and halved
1 carrot, quartered
1 leek, white part only, halved
1 stalk celery, quartered
1 clove garlic, peeled and crushed
5 sprigs fresh thyme, tied in a bundle
1 bay leaf, crushed
1 cup Puy lentils, washed under running water for 5 to 10 minutes
2 to 3 cups dark chicken stock (page 120)

TO FINISH LENTILS
1 Tbsp. unsalted butter
2 strips double-smoked bacon, finely diced
¼ tsp. minced garlic
1 shallot, peeled and finely diced
¼ cup finely diced carrot
¼ cup finely diced celery
½ cup dark chicken stock (page 120)
2 tsp. chopped fresh thyme leaves
1 tsp. chopped fresh Italian (flat-leaf) parsley

CARAMELIZED APPLES
2 small Gala apples
½ lemon, juice of
3 Tbsp. vegetable oil
1 Tbsp. honey

1 cup veal reduction (page 123)
Fleur de sel

TO MAKE DUCK CONFIT: Mix together garlic, bay leaf, thyme, coarse sea salt and peppercorns in a roasting pan. Rub the seasonings into duck legs and arrange them in one layer in the pan. Cover and refrigerate overnight.

Preheat the oven to 275°F.

Take out duck from the refrigerator. Under cold running water, rinse off spice mixture from duck and pat dry. Arrange duck in one layer in a non-aluminum roasting pan.

Melt duck fat (or lard) in a saucepan on medium heat and pour over duck legs, covering them completely. Cover the roasting pan with aluminum foil, shiny side in. Bake in the oven for 3 to 4 hours, or until the meat falls off the bone. Remove from the oven and allow duck to cool in the fat. Place duck legs in an airtight container and cover with duck fat strained through a fine-mesh sieve. Can be prepared ahead up to this point; will keep in the refrigerator for up to 2 weeks or in the freezer for up to 3 months.

LENTILS: Melt butter and olive oil in a saucepan on medium heat. Add bacon, shallot, carrot, leek, celery and garlic. Decrease the heat to low, cover saucepan and cook for about 5 minutes, or until vegetables are soft. Add thyme, bay leaf and lentils. Pour in enough stock to cover. Cover saucepan and simmer on medium heat, checking occasionally to ensure lentils are covered with stock. Keep adding stock as needed until lentils are tender, about 20 to 30 minutes. Remove from the heat. Take out and discard vegetables, herbs and bacon. Allow lentils to cool, then cover and refrigerate until needed.

CARAMELIZED APPLES: Peel and core apples. Cut each apple into 8 wedges and squeeze lemon juice over them to keep flesh from oxidizing.

Heat vegetable oil in a frying pan on medium heat. Add apple wedges and cook on both sides for about 3 minutes. Increase the heat to medium-high and add honey. Continue to cook until apples are dark golden brown and can easily be pierced with a knife. Remove from the heat and set aside.

TO ASSEMBLE: Preheat the oven to 350°F.

Remove duck legs from fat, wiping off excess with a paper towel, and place on a baking sheet. Place in the oven for 10 to 15 minutes to heat through and to crisp skin. Remove from the oven and keep warm.

To finish lentils, melt 1 teaspoon of the butter in a frying pan on medium heat. Sauté bacon, garlic, shallot, carrot and celery until soft. Add stock and cook until reduced by a third. Add lentils and cook for about 5 minutes, or until warmed through and nicely coated with stock. Add thyme, parsley and the remaining butter. Season to taste with salt and freshly ground white pepper. Keep warm.

Reheat caramelized apples in a microwave on high for 30 seconds or in the oven, alongside the duck legs, for 2 minutes, or until warmed thoroughly.

Heat veal reduction in a saucepan on medium heat and bring to a boil. Decrease the heat to low and keep warm.

Divide lentils among four warmed dinner plates. Arrange four slices of caramelized apple on each serving, then carefully place a duck leg on top. Spoon veal reduction over and around. Sprinkle duck with a little fleur de sel.

LUMIÈRE'S *Cassoulet*

I recently enjoyed eating cassoulet while on a trip to the south of France. A traditional cassoulet is always made with the constant staple of cannellini beans, but the type of meat added depends upon the region and what is available. Most people think of duck confit and sausages. Some people argue that it's the pork that makes a cassoulet, and others argue that it's the duck. This can be served as an appetizer or as a main course. *Serves 4*

BEANS
1½ cups dried cannellini beans, soaked in water overnight
1 stalk celery, quartered
½ onion, peeled and quartered

BOUQUET GARNI
6 sprigs fresh thyme
½ sprig fresh rosemary
5 black peppercorns
1 bay leaf

CASSOULET
1½ to 2 lbs. assorted sausages with medium fat content (bratwurst, lamb-mint, kielbasa, garlic)
1 lb. ham hock
2 tsp. olive oil
12 oz. sliced double-smoked bacon
½ cup ¼-inch dice onions
½ cup ¼-inch dice carrots
½ cup ¼-inch dice celery
2 tsp. minced garlic
½ cup dry white wine
1 Tbsp. molasses
4 Roma tomatoes, blanched, peeled and deseeded
⅔ cup canned Roma tomatoes
1½ cups dark chicken stock (page 120)
Rosemary oil (page 125)

TO MAKE BEANS: Drain presoaked beans and place in a large saucepan. Add enough fresh cold water to cover beans. Add celery and onion. Bring to a boil on medium heat. Remove from the heat, cover with a lid and allow to steep for 20 minutes.

BOUQUET GARNI: Take a 6-inch square piece of cheesecloth and in the centre place thyme, rosemary, peppercorns and bay leaf. Roll up cheesecloth loosely and tie closed with kitchen string. Set aside.

CASSOULET: Preheat the oven to 375°F.
Use a fork or a small knife to carefully pierce sausages. Sear sausages in a large frying pan on high heat until browned all over. Transfer to a large roasting pan. Cut

off meat from ham hock in 3-inch pieces; add meat and ham bone to the roasting pan. Set aside.

Heat olive oil in a large saucepan on medium heat. Sauté bacon, diced onions, carrots and celery for 5 to 10 minutes. Add garlic and continue to cook for 1 minute. Add wine and stir to deglaze the bottom of the pan. Drain beans, discarding water. Add beans, molasses, tomatoes, canned tomatoes, bouquet garni and stock. Continue to cook for another 5 minutes.

Pour bean mixture over browned sausages and ham in the roasting pan. Cover the roasting pan with aluminum foil (shiny side in) and pierce a couple of holes in it with a knife to allow the steam to escape. Bake in the oven for 1 to 1½ hours, or until beans are tender.

Remove from the oven, then pick out and discard ham bone and bouquet garni. Cut ham hock meat into 1- to 1½-inch pieces and return to beans. Cover and allow to rest for 15 minutes.

TO ASSEMBLE: Place 1 cup of beans in the centre of each of four warmed plates. Divide sausages and ham among the plates. Drizzle a little rosemary oil around the beans.

Bourbon Manhattan

2 oz. bourbon

½ oz. Italian (red) vermouth

½ oz. French (white) vermouth

3 dashes angostura bitters

. . .

Pour all ingredients into a
shaker full of cracked ice
and shake well. Strain into a
chilled cocktail glass.
Don't dare to sully it with a
maraschino cherry.

New York's Manhattan Club issued its bibular eponym in 1874, during a celebration of W.J. Tilden's gubernatorial victory. When the party's host (Winston Churchill's mother, according to legend) charged one of the resident barmen with creating a cocktail to mark the occasion, he generated a liquid icon that grew to challenge even the martini's popularity. Although Yankees may bristle at the inclusion of bourbon (instead insisting on the original rye), when the drink is made "perfect"—with equal amounts of sweet and dry vermouth—the result is a balanced, sweet-spicy aperitif with a surprising lightness.

MIXING TIPS: The Manhattan's recipe has been adapted ad infinitum: in place of the traditional rye, you can use brandy, rum or Scotch. The last is a Rob Roy, created to celebrate the 1894 Broadway opening of the same-named play.

CONFIT OF *Lamb* SHOULDER
WITH *Ratatouille*

We took the same concept as a traditional confit, but replaced the duck legs with lamb shoulder. The long slow cooking process makes the meat so tender that it will melt in your mouth. As in a classic confit, the fat not only preserves the meat for a long period of time but it also can be used again. The addition of ratatouille, with its great southern French flair, complements the flavour of the lamb. *Serves 4*

LAMB
2 to 3 lbs. lamb shoulder, deboned
¼ cup fresh thyme leaves
¼ cup fresh rosemary leaves
¼ cup fresh Italian (flat-leaf) parsley
1 clove garlic, peeled
¼ cup olive oil
6 to 8 cups rendered duck fat (page 127)
　 or lard
½ cup lamb stock (page 123)

RATATOUILLE
2 Tbsp. olive oil
1 red pepper, deseeded, 1-inch dice
1 yellow pepper, deseeded, 1-inch dice
1 zucchini, deseeded, 1-inch dice
1 eggplant, 1-inch dice
¾ tsp. minced garlic
2 tsp. ground cumin
¾ tsp. curry powder
⅓ cup lamb stock (page 123)

LAMB JUS
1½ cups lamb stock (page 123)
2 Tbsp. julienned fresh basil leaves

Fleur de sel for garnish

TO MAKE LAMB: Preheat the oven to 275°F.

Butterfly lamb shoulder. Remove and discard any tough sinew or fat.

Combine thyme, rosemary, parsley and garlic in a food processor and finely chop. Add olive oil and blend for 1 to 2 minutes. Season the inside of lamb shoulder with salt and freshly ground white pepper, then spread on herb mixture. Roll up lamb shoulder and tie with butcher's twine or kitchen string.

Place lamb in a small deep roasting pan. Melt duck fat (or lard) in a saucepan on low heat and pour into the roasting pan until lamb is completely immersed. Place the roasting pan on the stove-top on medium heat and bring duck fat (or lard) to a simmer. Cover pan with aluminum foil, shiny side in, and use a knife to pierce five or six holes to allow steam to escape. Then place in the oven and roast for 3½ to 4 hours, or until lamb is done (a skewer will pierce through the centre of the roast with no resistance). Take out of the oven and allow meat to cool in the fat in the roasting pan.

RATATOUILLE: Heat olive oil in a large saucepan on medium-high heat. Sauté red pepper, yellow pepper and zucchini until golden brown. Add eggplant and garlic, then cook for 5 minutes. Add ground cumin and curry powder, then cook for another 2 to 3 minutes. Add stock and cook until liquid is reduced by three quarters and eggplant is fork-tender. Season to taste with salt and freshly ground white pepper.

LAMB JUS: Place stock in a saucepan on high heat and simmer until reduced by one half, to intensify flavour. Season to taste with a little salt. Keep warm.

TO ASSEMBLE: Preheat the oven to 350°F.

Take lamb out of fat in the roasting pan; reserve fat for reuse. Remove the string and slice lamb into medallions 1½ inches thick. Heat a couple of tablespoons of the duck fat (or lard) in each of two large oven-proof frying pans on medium-high heat. Place two lamb medallions in each frying pan for about 1 minute per side, or until lightly browned. Add stock. Place lamb in the oven for about 5 minutes, then turn over and return to the oven for another 3 minutes. Lamb is ready when it is heated through and the stock glazes the meat.

Reheat ratatouille and divide among four warmed dinner plates. Place a medallion of lamb on top of each serving of ratatouille.

Add basil to warm lamb jus and spoon over lamb. Sprinkle each medallion with a little fleur de sel.

CÔTE DE *Boeuf* WITH ROASTED

PORTOBELLO MUSHROOMS AND *Bordelaise* SAUCE

*W*hen I was growing up, Sunday was my favourite day, because we always had roast beef. Usually it was prime rib—or as the French call it, *côte de boeuf*. This dish reminds me of those family meals. At the restaurant, we serve côte de boeuf with bordelaise sauce, one of the most classic sauces in French cuisine. *Serves 4*

CÔTE DE BOEUF

2 lbs. beef rib roast, on the bone
2 Tbsp. olive oil
1 Tbsp. coarsely ground black pepper
3 Tbsp. fleur de sel
3 Tbsp. vegetable oil

MUSHROOMS

8 medium portobello mushrooms
1 clove garlic, peeled and thinly sliced
8 sprigs fresh thyme
½ to 1 cup olive oil

BORDELAISE SAUCE

¾ cup dry red wine
⅓ cup ruby port
½ cup shallots, peeled and finely sliced
4 cloves garlic, peeled
2 sprigs fresh thyme
4 cups veal reduction (page 123)
1 Tbsp. unsalted butter

Fleur de sel for garnish

TO MAKE CÔTE DE BOEUF: Preheat the oven to 400°F.

Trim off excess fat from beef. (Reserve the trimmings for making short stock, page 124, or for another use.) Coat beef with olive oil. Season with black pepper and fleur de sel, pressing into the meat with your fingers. Tie butcher's twine or kitchen string around the roast to help it keep its shape during cooking.

Heat vegetable oil in a large cast-iron skillet on high heat. Sear beef on all sides until dark brown. Transfer to a roasting pan and roast in the oven for 10 minutes. Turn beef over and continue to cook for another 15 to 20 minutes, or until desired doneness. Remove from the oven, but leave oven on. Allow meat to rest for 10 minutes before carving.

MUSHROOMS: Remove and discard stems and gills from mushrooms. Place mushroom caps, cut side up, in an oven-proof pan. Sprinkle with sliced garlic and place a sprig of thyme on each cap. Generously pour olive oil on mushrooms to coat caps, then season with salt and freshly ground white pepper. Roast in the oven for about 10 minutes, or until tender. Remove from the oven and allow to cool. Remove and discard garlic and thyme.

BORDELAISE SAUCE: Combine wine and port in a saucepan on medium heat. Add shallots, garlic and thyme. Cook until liq-uid is reduced to a syrup. Add veal reduction and cook until reduced by one third. Remove from the heat and stir in butter. Strain through a fine-mesh strainer into a clean saucepan and keep warm.

TO ASSEMBLE: Carve meat from the bone. Place two portobello mushrooms on each plate. Place a few slices of carved beef to the side of the mushrooms on each plate and sprinkle with a little fleur de sel. Serve warm sauce on the side.

Chocolate Fondant with
Honey Tangerine Marmalade and
India Spice Ice Cream / 84

Chocolate Pecan Phyllo Tart
with Red Wine and Orange Caramel
Ice Cream / 88

Milk Chocolate Mousse and Pumpkin
Sponge Cake with Sour Cream Mousse
and Candied Pumpkin Seeds / 91

Chocolate Trio: Chocolate Brownie,
Chocolate Mousse and Chocolate
Fleur de Sel Meringue / 94

Caramelized Banana Bread Pudding
with Honey Buttermilk Sorbet and
Rum Caramel Sauce / 99

Gingerbread Cake with Chocolate-
Cinnamon Crème Anglaise and
Sweet Potato Ice Cream / 102

Lemon Coeur à la Crème with
Lemon Sauce / 104

Goat Cheese Tart with Port Reduction
and Candied Mixed Nuts / 108

Passion Fruit Soufflé with
Chocolate Sauce / 110

Blackberries in Moscato with Lemon
Verbena Anglaise, Vanilla Cream and
Lime Zest Wafer / 112

Baby Banana in Shredded Phyllo with
Coconut-Chocolate Ice Cream / 115

Rice Pudding with Vanilla-stewed
Rhubarb / 117

Desserts

CHOCOLATE *Fondant* WITH HONEY TANGERINE
MARMALADE AND *India Spice* ICE CREAM

O n one of my many trips to New York, I had a wonderful warm chocolate fondant with an almost liquid centre. We serve it with a honey tangerine marmalade whose acidity and tartness plays off the rich chocolate beautifully. The ice cream adds the elements of spice and cream.

The turbinado sugar we use in the marmalade is a coarse sugar that is light brown in colour because it contains molasses. You'll find it at specialty or health food stores. *Serves 8*

INDIA SPICE ICE CREAM

1 cup heavy cream
1 cup light cream or half-and-half
½ cup granulated sugar
2 tsp. black tea leaves
½ cinnamon stick
2 star anise
2 tsp. fennel seeds
3 cardamom pods
3 whole cloves
½ vanilla bean, split and pulp scraped
5 large egg yolks
1 tsp. fresh lemon juice

MARMALADE

8 honey tangerines
1 cup turbinado sugar
½ vanilla bean, split and pulp scraped
1 Tbsp. Grand Marnier

CHOCOLATE FONDANT

½ cup unsalted butter
4 oz. bittersweet chocolate, ¼-inch pieces
2 large eggs
2 large egg yolks
¼ cup granulated sugar
1 Tbsp. all-purpose flour

TO MAKE ICE CREAM: Combine heavy cream, light cream (or half-and-half) and ¼ cup of the sugar in a saucepan on medium-high heat; bring just to a boil. Stir in tea leaves, cinnamon stick, star anise, fennel seeds, cardamom, cloves and vanilla bean pulp and pod. Remove from the heat, cover and allow to infuse for 1 hour.

Return infused cream to the stove on medium-high heat and bring back just to a boil. Remove from the heat and strain through a fine-mesh sieve, discarding spices.

In a bowl, whisk together egg yolks and the remaining ¼ cup of the sugar until light and fluffy. Temper egg mixture by whisking in a small amount of the infused cream, then slowly stir in the rest of the cream. Transfer to a clean saucepan and return to medium heat, stirring constantly with a wooden spoon until it reaches 175°F on a candy thermometer or coats the back of a spoon. Do not boil or overcook, else it will curdle. Stir in lemon juice.

Strain through a fine-mesh sieve into a stainless steel bowl placed over a bowl of ice to stop the cooking. Allow to cool.

Place the mixture in an ice-cream maker and process according to the manufacturer's instructions. Freeze until ready to use. Makes 2 cups. Will keep in the freezer for up to 1 month.

MARMALADE: Remove peel from honey tangerines. Use a knife to carefully scrape off half of the pith from the inside of the peel and discard pith. Cut the cleaned peel into small thin strips. Use a sharp knife to cut and remove the tangerine segments, then squeeze the remaining membrane to extract any juice.

Combine thinly cut peel, tangerine segments and juice with turbinado sugar, vanilla bean pulp and pod in a saucepan on medium heat. Bring mixture to a boil, then decrease the heat to medium-low and simmer, stirring occasionally, for about 20 minutes until slightly thickened. Remove vanilla bean pod and stir in Grand Marnier. Transfer marmalade to a glass container and allow to cool. Cover and refrigerate until ready to use. Will keep in the refrigerator for 1 week and in the freezer for up to 1 month.

CHOCOLATE FONDANT: Melt butter and chocolate in the top of a double boiler set over simmering water, mixing well. Remove from the heat.

Combine eggs, egg yolks and sugar in the top of another double boiler or in a stainless steel bowl over simmering water. Use a kitchen mixer or a whisk to beat egg mixture until it doubles in volume. Remove from the heat (the gentle heat gives more volume to the mixture).

When egg mixture is partially cooled, fold one third of it into the melted chocolate. Add the remaining egg mixture to the melted chocolate. Sift in flour and fold into mixture until fully incorporated. Cover and refrigerate until ready to use.

TO ASSEMBLE: Preheat the oven to 375°F. Butter eight ring molds 3 inches in diameter and place them on a parchment-lined baking sheet. Spoon chocolate fondant batter into the molds, filling each no more than three quarters full. Bake in the oven for 8 to 10 minutes, or until tops are slightly puffed.

Use a small knife to cut carefully cut around the inside edges of the molds. Remove the chocolate fondant cakes from the molds and place them on individual plates. Place a spoonful of honey tangerine marmalade at the side and top each cake with a scoop of India spice ice cream.

Pisco Sour

South America's spicy antipode to the whiskey sour, built from their fierce muscat brandy, pisco, adds zest to any occasion. A summer staple in Chile and Peru, the drink was likely inspired in the 1920s by visiting American and European steamship passengers who incorporated the native spirit into the popular sour formula. The best pisco sours are made *a lo peruano*—in the Peruvian style—with a few dashes of angostura bitters to add subtle notes of cinnamon and cloves, and a dollop of egg white to affix a frothy head.

MIXING TIPS: *Limons de pica*, the citrus fruit traditionally used to make this drink, are difficult to find in North America. A mixture of half lemon and half lime juice makes an acceptable substitute. Be sure to shake this drink hard for 20 to 30 seconds to whip the egg white into a meringue-like head.

2 oz. pisco

½ oz. simple syrup for cocktails
(page 126)

½ oz. fresh lemon juice

½ oz. fresh lime juice

3 dashes angostura bitters

1 fresh egg white

· · ·

Pour all ingredients into a shaker full of cracked ice and shake hard for 20 to 30 seconds. Strain into a chilled sour glass.

CHOCOLATE PECAN *Phyllo Tart* WITH RED WINE AND ORANGE *Caramel* ICE CREAM

*E*veryone knows that chocolate and pecans naturally go well together. But the combination of red wine and chocolate is a pairing that I learned about several years ago from a Vancouver wine writer. The red wine and orange flavours of the ice cream came into being from a base that we originally used for a duck sauce. Our pastry chef, Marcia Kurbis, incorporated this reduction into a crème anglaise to make this unique ice cream. It complements the rich and gooey chocolate pecan tart wonderfully. *Serves 8*

RED WINE AND ORANGE CARAMEL ICE CREAM

¾ cup granulated sugar
¼ cup water
½ cup dry red wine
2 oranges, zest and juice separate
3 cups heavy cream
1 cup milk
8 egg yolks
½ cup granulated sugar

FILLING

2 eggs
⅓ cup granulated sugar
2 tsp. Grand Marnier
3 Tbsp. unsalted butter, melted
3 tsp. heavy cream
¾ cup light corn syrup
1 cup pecans, toasted and roughly chopped
6 oz. bittersweet chocolate, ¼-inch pieces

TART SHELLS

6 sheets frozen phyllo, thawed
2 cups unsalted butter, melted
½ cup turbinado sugar (page 84)

TANGERINE JUS

2 cups fresh tangerine juice
¼ to ½ cup granulated sugar
¼ cup Grand Marnier
½ vanilla bean, split and pulp scraped

TO MAKE ICE CREAM: Place the ¾ cup of sugar and water in a heavy-bottomed saucepan on medium heat until light amber in colour. Remove from the heat and carefully whisk in red wine and orange juice. Allow to cool and set aside.

In another saucepan on medium heat, combine cream and milk and bring just to a boil. Remove from the heat.

Whisk together egg yolks and the ½ cup of sugar in a bowl, until light and fluffy. Temper egg mixture by whisking in a small amount of the warm cream, then slowly add the rest of the cream.

Strain through a fine-mesh sieve into a clean saucepan and return to the heat, stirring constantly with a wooden spoon. Bring to 175°F on a candy thermometer, or until the sauce coats the back of the spoon. Do not boil or overcook, as it will curdle.

Remove from the heat and whisk in red wine mixture. Immediately strain through a fine-mesh sieve into a clean stainless steel bowl placed over a bowl of ice to stop the cooking, and allow to cool. Stir in orange zest. When cool, cover and refrigerate until ready to process.

Place mixture in an ice-cream maker and process according to the manufacturer's instructions. Freeze until ready to use. Makes 4 cups. Will keep in the freezer for up to 1 month.

FILLING: Whisk together eggs and sugar in a bowl. Add Grand Marnier, melted butter, cream, corn syrup, pecans and chocolate. Mix well. Cover and refrigerate until ready to use.

TART SHELLS: Preheat the oven to 325°F.

Lay one sheet of phyllo on a clean surface. Use a pastry brush to gently dust off flour from both sides of phyllo. Use another pastry brush to coat one side of the phyllo with a little melted butter, then sprinkle with a little of the sugar. Repeat this process for all six sheets of phyllo.

Stack three phyllo sheets on top of each other to form two stacks with three sheets in each.

Cut each of the two phyllo stacks into four 6½-inch squares, to end up with eight squares. Fit each phyllo square into one of eight 4-inch diameter tart molds. Place the phyllo-lined tart molds on a baking sheet and bake in the oven for 10 minutes. Remove from the oven but leave the oven on. Allow tart shells to cool in their molds.

TANGERINE JUS: Combine tangerine juice, sugar, Grand Marnier, and vanilla bean pulp and pod in a saucepan on medium-high heat. Cook until reduced by two thirds. Strain through a fine-mesh sieve and cool.

TO ASSEMBLE: Divide filling among tart shells, still in their molds, and return to the oven. Bake for 20 to 25 minutes, until filling is firm to the touch.

Drizzle 1 teaspoon of tangerine jus just off centre on each of eight dessert plates. Remove tarts from molds and place one on each plate to the side of the jus. Top each tart with a scoop of ice cream.

< MILK CHOCOLATE MOUSSE AND *Pumpkin* SPONGE CAKE
WITH SOUR CREAM MOUSSE AND *Candied* PUMPKIN SEEDS

*T*he tartness of the sour cream mousse cuts through the richness of the chocolate. And the pumpkin and chocolate make an interesting match, much like zucchini and chocolate, yet complement each other well. Not only that, but you can make this dessert ahead and freeze it.
Serves 8 to 10

CAKE
⅔ cup cake flour
1½ tsp. ground cinnamon
½ tsp. baking powder
¼ tsp. ground nutmeg
¼ tsp. ground allspice
2 large eggs
1¼ cups packed Demerara sugar
¼ cup granulated sugar
1 cup canned good quality pure pumpkin
  purée
2 Tbsp. finely chopped candied ginger

MILK CHOCOLATE MOUSSE
30 oz. milk chocolate, ¼-inch pieces
1 cup milk
1 cup heavy cream
1 Tbsp. light corn syrup
2 cups heavy cream, whipped to
  soft peaks

SOUR CREAM MOUSSE
¾ cup heavy cream
½ vanilla bean, pulp only
1 tsp. icing sugar
1 gelatin leaf
¾ cup sour cream

PUMPKIN SEEDS
1 cup raw shelled pumpkin seeds
¼ cup simple syrup (page 126)

TO MAKE CAKE: Preheat the oven to 350°F.

Sift together flour, ground cinnamon, baking powder, ground nutmeg and ground allspice into a bowl. Set aside.

In a kitchen mixer with a whisk attachment, beat eggs with Demerara and granulated sugar until fluffy. Mix in pumpkin purée. Fold in the sifted dry ingredients and candied ginger. The batter should be quite thin.

Butter and flour an 11 × 17-inch baking sheet, then line with parchment paper (this will help to prevent the centre from sticking so that the cake can be removed in one piece). Turn out batter onto the parchment and spread out evenly. Bake in the oven for 10 to 15 minutes, or until done (a toothpick inserted into the centre will come out clean). Remove from the oven and allow to cool.

continued overleaf >

When the cake has cooled, place a 9 × 13-inch rectangular cake pan on top of it and use a sharp knife to cut around the edge of the cake pan. (Cake can be made ahead of time. Wrapped tightly in plastic wrap, it will keep in the freezer for up to 1 month.)

MILK CHOCOLATE MOUSSE: Place chopped chocolate in a large stainless steel bowl.

Combine milk, cream and corn syrup in a saucepan on medium heat and bring to a boil. Pour over milk chocolate and stir until it melts. Allow to cool for 5 minutes, then fold in whipped cream.

Pour chocolate mousse into a 9 × 13-inch rectangular cake pan lined with plastic wrap. Place cake on top of mousse and press gently to ensure a tight fit. Refrigerate for 8 hours, or until mousse has completely set. (The mousse cake can be made ahead; will keep in the refrigerator for 4 days, in the freezer for up to 1 month.)

SOUR CREAM MOUSSE: Combine heavy cream, vanilla bean pulp and icing sugar in a chilled bowl; whip until it reaches stiff peaks. (Save vanilla bean pod for another use.) Cover and refrigerate until needed.

Place gelatin leaf in a bowl and cover with cold water. Allow to sit for about 1 minute to soften.

Place three quarters of the sour cream in a bowl and set aside.

Place the remaining quarter of the sour cream in a saucepan on low heat and warm gently. Take out gelatin leaf from the cold water and squeeze gently to remove any excess water. Remove sour cream from the heat and add softened gelatin leaf, stirring until it dissolves. Quickly fold gelatin mixture into the remaining sour cream. Fold this mixture into whipped vanilla cream. Cover and refrigerate until needed.

PUMPKIN SEEDS: Preheat the oven to 350°F.

Toss pumpkin seeds with simple syrup in a bowl, until seeds are well coated. Spread on a parchment-lined baking sheet and bake in the oven for 5 to 7 minutes, or until pumpkin seeds are nicely toasted and slightly puffed.

TO ASSEMBLE: Place a parchment-lined baking sheet over the open top of the cake pan. In one motion, turn over both the baking sheet and the pan together, so that the baking sheet is on the bottom. Gently pull off the cake pan while pulling down on the plastic wrap to release the mousse cake. Remove and discard the plastic wrap.

Use a warmed knife to cut the mousse cake into 2½-inch squares. Top each square with a small dollop of sour cream mousse and some candied pumpkin seeds.

Chocolate Trio: CHOCOLATE BROWNIE, CHOCOLATE MOUSSE AND CHOCOLATE FLEUR DE SEL Meringue

What could be more heavenly for a chocolate fanatic than a trio of chocolate desserts? I love this dessert because it also is a trio of textures: the chocolate brownie is very dense and moist, the chocolate mousse is very light and soft, and the salted chocolate meringue adds crunch. Don't worry about the sprinkle of salt on the meringue—I think that salt and chocolate is truly a magical pairing. *Serves 6 to 8*

MERINGUE
2 to 3 Tbsp. cocoa powder
1 tsp. cornstarch
4 large eggs, whites only
1 cup berry sugar
½ tsp. white vinegar
Fleur de sel or coarse sea salt

BROWNIES
1 cup all-purpose flour
½ tsp. salt
⅛ cup cocoa powder
8 oz. dark chocolate, ¼-inch pieces
1 cup unsalted butter
4 eggs
2 cups granulated sugar
1½ tsp. vanilla extract

MOUSSE
1½ cups heavy cream
9 oz. dark chocolate, ¼-inch pieces
½ cup granulated sugar
4 to 5 Tbsp. cold water
5 egg yolks
1 egg

TO MAKE MERINGUE: Preheat the oven to 250°F.

Sift together cocoa powder and cornstarch into a bowl.

Place egg whites in a kitchen mixer with a whisk attachment. Whisk on medium speed for 1 minute. Gradually beat in berry sugar. Add vinegar and continue to beat until egg whites form stiff peaks. Gently fold in cocoa mixture.

Spread meringue into six to eight rounds, 3 inches in diameter and ⅛ inch thick, on a parchment-lined baking sheet. Sprinkle the tops with a little fleur de sel (or coarse sea salt). Bake in the oven for about 1 hour, or until crisp. Remove from the oven and allow to cool to room temperature. Place in an airtight container until ready to use; will keep for 2 days.

BROWNIES: Preheat the oven to 350°F.

Sift together flour, salt and cocoa into a bowl.

Melt together chocolate and butter in the top of a double boiler over simmering water.

Beat eggs in a kitchen mixer with a whisk attachment for 4 minutes at medium speed, then gradually add half of the sugar. Add vanilla extract. Add the remaining sugar and mix well. Temper the egg mixture by stirring in ½ cup of the warm melted chocolate, then stir in the remaining melted chocolate. Fold in the flour mixture.

Spread the batter out evenly on a parchment-lined 11 × 17-inch baking sheet. Bake in the oven for about 35 minutes, or until done (the middle springs back when gently pressed with your finger). Remove from the oven and allow to cool. Remove from the baking sheet, wrap in plastic wrap and refrigerate until ready to use. Will keep for 1 week in the refrigerator or in the freezer for up to 2 months.

MOUSSE: Place cream in a chilled bowl and whip until soft peaks form. Cover and refrigerate until needed.

Melt chocolate in a double boiler or in a stainless steel bowl over a bowl of simmering water and keep warm.

Combine sugar and cold water in a heavy-bottomed saucepan, mixing just until sugar is moistened. Place the saucepan on low heat and cook until sugar is dissolved. Increase the heat to medium and bring to a boil. The sugar should read 240°F on a candy thermometer and be at the soft ball stage. (To test for the soft ball stage, dip a metal spoon into the hot sugar and then into a bowl of ice water. The sugar should form a sticky ball when rolled between your fingers.) Keep sugar warm.

Beat egg yolks and egg in a kitchen mixer with a whisk attachment on medium speed for 2 to 3 minutes. Slowly whisk in sugar, pouring it down the side of the bowl to prevent it from splattering everywhere. When sugar is all incorporated, continue to whisk until mixture triples in volume. Stop whisking and temper egg mixture by adding a quarter of the warm melted chocolate, then gently fold in the rest of the chocolate.

Take out whipped cream from the refrigerator and whisk until stiff peaks form. Gently fold one third of the whipped cream into the chocolate mixture, then fold in the rest of the whipped cream. Cover with plastic wrap and refrigerate for at least 1 hour.

TO ASSEMBLE: Cut brownie into 2-inch squares and place one in the middle of each of six to eight dessert plates. Place a heaping tablespoon of mousse on top of each brownie and finish with a chocolate meringue disk on top of the mousse.

Sazerac

Sugar cube

2 dashes Peychaud's Bitters

1 dash angostura bitters

2 oz. rye

Dash of absinthe

Lemon

. . .

Place sugar cube in a mixer
and soak with Peychaud's
and angostura bitters.
Add rye and stir with a
barspoon until the sugar is
mostly dissolved.
Add absinthe to a chilled
rocks glass and rinse glass
thoroughly with it.
Pour contents of the mixer
into a shaker full of cracked ice
and shake well. Strain
into the rocks glass. Zest a
lemon over the glass
and drop in the twist or not,
according to taste.

First mixed in the 1850s, the Sazerac is widely considered to be the oldest cocktail in the Americas. Antoine Peychaud, noted New Orleans apothecary and vendor of healing tonics, devised the original recipe to aid sales of his medicinal bitters. In the late 1850s, the importers of Sazerac cognac opened the Sazerac House and featured this cocktail. Rye and bourbon eventually replaced the brandy, and then absinthe—the Impressionists' muse—was added to give the drink greater depth. After absinthe was outlawed in the U.S., the local pastis Herbsaint was used. While tastes and the drink's recipe have changed appreciably since the Sazerac's creation, its rejuvenating powers have remained constant.

MIXING TIPS: Use any pastis such as Ricard, Pernod or Herbsaint as a substitute for the absinthe. A teaspoon of sugar will work in place of the cube.

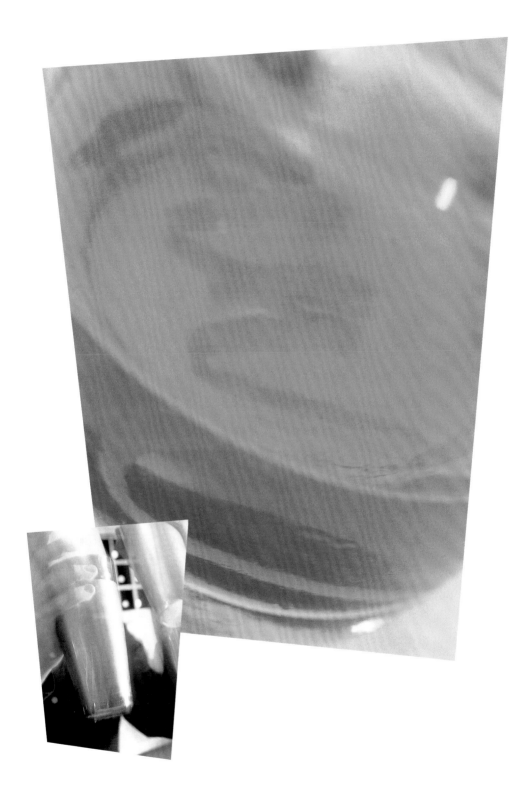

CARAMELIZED *Banana* BREAD PUDDING WITH HONEY BUTTERMILK *Sorbet* AND RUM CARAMEL SAUCE

This dessert is a variation of a New Orleans–style bread pudding. Typically, it is caramelized on the top layer and is often served with Bananas Foster and crème anglaise. Our pastry chef, Marcia Kurbis, decided to combine all of these elements into one creation. The end result is a rich hot and cold dessert that reminds me of the bread pudding my mother used to make. *Serves 8*

HONEY BUTTERMILK SORBET
⅓ cup honey
¼ cup light corn syrup
2 cups buttermilk

CARAMEL
1 cup granulated sugar

CARAMEL SAUCE
2 cups granulated sugar
1 cup heavy cream
½ cup dark rum
Pinch of salt

CUSTARD
2 cups milk
1 cinnamon stick
1 vanilla bean, split and pulp scraped
5 whole eggs
½ cup granulated sugar

BANANA BREAD
½ cup unsalted butter
2 loaves French bread (stale, 1 day old)
Freshly ground cinnamon
Freshly ground nutmeg
1 banana

TO MAKE HONEY BUTTERMILK SORBET: Warm honey and corn syrup together in a saucepan on medium heat for about 3 minutes, or in a bowl in the microwave for about 30 seconds on high heat, or until melted and easy to pour. Whisk into buttermilk. Freeze in an ice-cream maker according to the manufacturer's instructions. Makes 2 cups. Will keep in the freezer for up to 1 month.

CARAMEL: Melt 1 tablespoon of the sugar in a heavy-bottomed saucepan on medium-high heat. While stirring constantly, add 1 tablespoon of the sugar at a time, until all is melted. Continue to cook until sugar turns light amber. Remove from the heat and carefully pour caramel into a 5 × 9-inch loaf pan, making sure you cover the bottom evenly. Set aside and allow to cool.

CARAMEL SAUCE: Melt 1 tablespoon of the sugar in a heavy-bottomed saucepan on medium-high heat. While stirring constantly, add 1 tablespoon of the sugar at a time until all is melted. Continue to cook until it turns dark amber.

Remove from the heat and carefully whisk in cream. Return to the heat and cook for another 2 minutes. Remove from the heat and add rum and salt. Strain through a fine-mesh sieve and allow to cool.

continued overleaf >

CUSTARD: Place milk, cinnamon stick, vanilla bean pulp and pod in a saucepan on medium heat. Bring to a boil. Remove from the heat and set aside.

In a stainless steel bowl, whisk together eggs and sugar until light and fluffy. Temper the egg mixture by whisking in ½ cup of the warm milk mixture. Whisk in the remainder of the warm milk, and transfer vanilla bean pod and cinnamon stick into mixture to infuse the flavours. Cool, then strain through a fine-mesh sieve. Set aside.

TO ASSEMBLE: Preheat the oven to 350°F.

Use some of the butter to grease the sides of the loaf pan that has the caramel in the bottom. Cut off and discard the crusts from both loaves of French bread. Cut off a few ¾-inch thick slices to line the bottom of the loaf pan and fit very tightly inside. Cut the remainder of bread into 1-inch cubes and set aside.

Dot the bottom layer of bread with 2 tablespoons of the butter. Sprinkle with some cinnamon and nutmeg. Drizzle with 2 to 3 tablespoons of the caramel sauce.

Peel banana and slice lengthwise to make long strips ¼ inch thick. Lay a couple of banana slices on top of bread slices. Pack in a layer of bread cubes, then pour 2 to 2½ cups of custard over top. Gently press down to help bread to absorb custard.

Repeat butter, cinnamon, nutmeg, caramel sauce, banana, bread cubes and custard until the loaf pan is full. Use your hands to press down gently on the top to ensure that all ingredients are incorporated together. The custard should not spill over the top but should be fully absorbed into the bread, giving it a sponge-like feel and a dense texture.

Cut a piece of aluminum foil that is double the width of the loaf pan. Fold it in half and butter one side. Place the foil over the loaf pan, buttered side down, and seal tightly to the pan.

Place the loaf pan in a roasting pan. Pour hot water into the roasting pan until it reaches three quarters up the sides of the loaf pan. Bake in the oven for 1½ to 2 hours. When done, the banana bread pudding should be slightly puffed and firm to the touch in the centre. Remove from the oven and allow to rest for 10 to 15 minutes.

Run a small knife around the inside edges of the loaf pan and invert the pudding onto a flat surface. To help the pudding to slide out, gently tap the bottom of the loaf pan to break the suction that has been created during baking. Place the pudding in an airtight container and refrigerate. Will keep for up to 4 days.

TO SERVE: Cut pudding into eight portions and place on separate plates. Heat individual portions in the microwave for 30 seconds on high. Heat caramel sauce and pour ¼ cup over each serving. Place a scoop of honey buttermilk sorbet on top of the pudding or on the side of each plate.

GINGERBREAD *Cake* WITH CHOCOLATE-CINNAMON CRÈME ANGLAISE AND *Sweet Potato* ICE CREAM

There is nothing more appealing than coming in from a cold winter day to the lovely aroma of gingerbread. Our pastry chef, Marcia Kurbis, came up with this unusual sweet potato ice cream, which was created from what had originally been the base for a sweet potato pecan pie.
Serves 8 to 10

SWEET POTATO ICE CREAM
3 medium sweet potatoes
¼ cup Demerara sugar
1 Tbsp. vanilla extract
¼ tsp. salt
¼ tsp. ground cinnamon
⅛ tsp. ground allspice
⅛ tsp ground nutmeg
⅓ cup dark rum
3 cups heavy cream
1 cup milk
8 egg yolks
1 cup granulated sugar

CAKE
¾ cup dark fancy grade molasses
1 tsp. baking soda
1½ cups boiling water
¼ cup unsalted butter, softened
1 cup packed Demerara sugar
1 egg
4½ tsp. finely grated fresh ginger
2½ cups all-purpose flour
1 Tbsp. baking powder
½ tsp. salt
1 Tbsp. ground ginger
1½ tsp. ground cinnamon
Pinch of ground cloves

CRÈME ANGLAISE
1 cup milk
3 egg yolks
¼ cup granulated sugar
1 oz. bittersweet chocolate, melted
½ tsp. ground cinnamon

TO MAKE ICE CREAM: Preheat the oven to 350°F.

Use a fork to pierce the skin of each sweet potato a few times, then arrange them on a baking sheet. Bake in the oven for about 1 hour, or until soft. Take out of the oven and allow to cool slightly. Remove and discard skin from sweet potatoes, reserving potato flesh.

Purée 1 cup of the sweet potato flesh with Demerara sugar, vanilla extract, salt, ground cinnamon, ground allspice, ground nutmeg and dark rum in a food processor or blender. Strain through a fine-mesh sieve.

Combine cream and milk in a saucepan on medium heat and bring just to a boil. Remove from the heat.

Whisk together egg yolks and sugar in a bowl, until light and fluffy. Temper egg mixture by whisking in a small amount of the warm cream, then slowly add the rest of the cream.

Strain through a fine-mesh sieve into a clean saucepan and return to the heat, stirring constantly with a wooden spoon. Bring to 175°F on a candy thermometer, or until the sauce coats the back of the spoon. Do not boil or overcook, as it will curdle.

Stir in sweet potato purée and mix thoroughly. Remove from the heat and immediately strain through a fine-mesh sieve into a clean stainless steel bowl placed over a bowl of ice to stop the cooking. Allow to cool.

Place the mixture in an ice-cream maker and process according to the manufacturer's instructions. Freeze until ready to use. Makes 4 cups. Will keep in the freezer for up to 1 month.

CAKE: Preheat the oven to 350°F.

Place molasses and baking soda in a stainless steel bowl. Pour in boiling water. Whisk together and allow to cool.

Place butter and Demerara sugar in a kitchen mixer with a paddle attachment and cream together at medium speed until light and fluffy. Add egg and ginger. Scrape down the sides of the bowl and mix for another 2 minutes. Transfer mixture to a large bowl.

In another bowl, sift together flour, baking powder, salt, ground ginger, ground cinnamon and ground cloves. Alternating between wet and dry ingredients, stir molasses mixture and flour mixture into the creamed butter, ⅓ cup of each at a time.

Pour the batter into a buttered, floured and parchment-lined 9 × 13-inch rectangular cake pan. Bake in the oven for 20 minutes, then decrease the heat to 325°F and continue to bake for a further 10 to 15

minutes, or until done. (Cake is done when a toothpick inserted into the centre pulls out clean.) Remove from the oven and allow to cool or serve warm.

CRÈME ANGLAISE: Place milk in a saucepan on medium heat and bring just to a boil. Remove from the heat, but leave the burner on.

Whisk together egg yolks and sugar in a bowl, until light and fluffy. Temper egg mixture by whisking in a small amount of the warm milk, then slowly add the rest of the milk.

Strain through a fine-mesh sieve into a clean saucepan and return to the heat, stirring constantly with a wooden spoon. Bring to 175°F on a candy thermometer, or until the sauce coats the back of the spoon. Do not boil or overcook, as it will curdle. Add melted chocolate and ground cinnamon. Remove from the heat and immediately strain through a fine-mesh sieve into a clean stainless steel bowl placed over a bowl of ice to the stop cooking. Allow to cool. Cover and refrigerate until ready to use.

TO ASSEMBLE: Cut the gingerbread cake into 2½-inch squares. Place 2 tablespoons of crème anglaise in the centre of each of eight to ten dessert plates and top with a slice of cake. Place a scoop of sweet potato ice cream beside each piece of cake.

LEMON *Coeur* À LA CRÈME
WITH *Lemon* SAUCE

This dessert is derived from the classic French version of *coeur à la crème*—which, in English, means "heart of the cream." Typically, a fresh cheese (fromage blanc) is made from a combination of yogurt and cottage cheese processed together with lemon juice. This "cheese" is then poured into a cheesecloth-lined, heart-shaped "coeur" mold, which has holes in the bottom to allow the whey to drain out. Coeur à la crème is usually served with fresh berries.

For more richness, we use a combination of fromage blanc, whipped cream and mascarpone. The lemon sauce both complements and cuts through the richly decadent cheese. *Serves 6*

COEUR À LA CRÈME
½ cup turbinado sugar (page 84)
¼ cup fresh lemon juice
½ cup heavy cream
½ vanilla bean, pulp only
2 cups mascarpone
1 cup fromage blanc (page 127)

SAUCE
6 egg yolks
1¼ cups granulated sugar
½ cup + 1 Tbsp. fresh lemon juice
⅓ cup unsalted butter

TO MAKE COEUR À LA CRÈME:
Combine turbinado sugar and lemon juice in a saucepan on medium heat and cook until it reaches 220°F on a candy thermometer. Remove lemon syrup from the heat and allow to cool. Set aside.

Cut six squares of cheesecloth 5 × 5 inches, large enough to line the insides of six 6-ounce ramekins with an extra 1 inch to cover. Soak cheesecloth in ice water for at least 25 minutes.

Combine cream and vanilla bean pulp in a chilled bowl, then whip until cream reaches soft peaks. (Save vanilla bean pod for another use.)

In another bowl, gently stir mascarpone to soften it. Slowly incorporate fromage blanc, stirring gently to ensure there are no lumps. Drizzle in the reserved lemon syrup and mix well. Fold in whipped vanilla cream.

Squeeze excess water from the cheesecloth squares and fit tightly into ramekins, ensuring that all of the inside surfaces are covered, with 1 inch excess over the sides.

Spoon coeur à la crème into ramekins until full. Fold the excess cheesecloth over the top of the filled ramekins and gently push down on the top to ensure that the coeur à la crème takes the shape of the ramekins. Refrigerate for at least 6 hours.

LEMON SAUCE: Whisk all ingredients together in stainless steel bowl over a bowl of simmering water or in a double boiler on medium heat. Cook for about 20 minutes, stirring occasionally, until thick enough to coat the back of a spoon. Place over a bowl of ice to stop the cooking. Allow to cool, then strain through a fine-mesh sieve. Place in a covered container and refrigerate until ready to use.

TO ASSEMBLE: Undo the cheesecloth at the top of each ramekin. Invert each ramekin onto an individual chilled plate, gently lifting up ramekin and pulling down on the cheesecloth to free the coeurs à la crème. Pour 1 or 2 tablespoons of lemon sauce over each one.

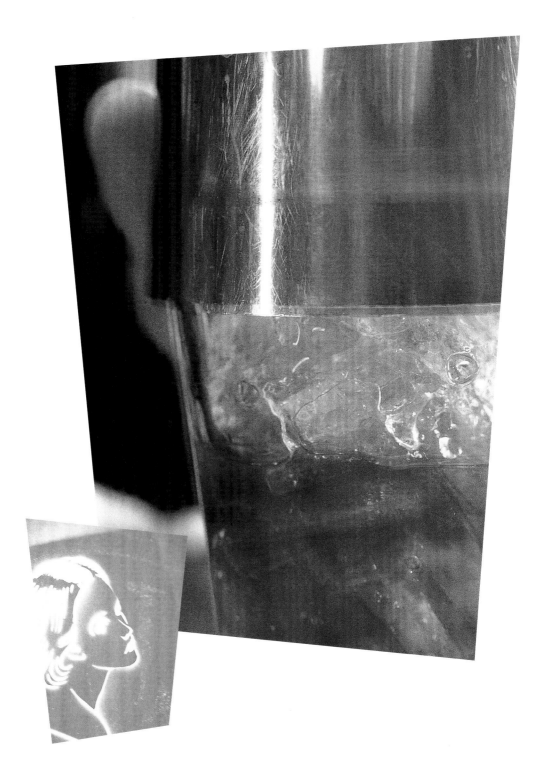

Mulatto

Much has changed in Havana since Papa Hemingway famously quaffed daiquiris there in the 1940s. Long gone are the days when Prohibition turned Cuba's capital into the playground of American revellers (Meyer Lansky and Lucky Luciano among them) eager to escape the austere laws back home. Today, in the Rampa quarter of Havana, some of Cuba's best night spots lie nestled among the faded forms of Jazz Age casinos and crumbling Mafia hotels. The island's cocktail culture has also endured. On a recent visit to one of the area's premier jazz clubs, La Zorra y El Cuervo, the Mulatto was discovered: a dark daiquiri with a bedevilling hint of chocolate.

MIXING TIPS: The trick to mixing a great Mulatto is not to be heavy handed with the crème de cacao. Too much chocolate liqueur and the drink will be a sticky mess, but when made properly, the chocolate complements the caramel hues of the dark rum and is just detectable on the finish.

2 oz. dark rum

1 dash simple syrup for cocktails (page 126)

1 dash crème de cacao

1 oz. fresh lime juice

. . .

Pour all ingredients into a shaker full of cracked ice and shake well. Strain into a chilled cocktail glass.

GOAT CHEESE *Tart* WITH PORT REDUCTION AND *Candied* MIXED NUTS

Three main flavour components make this dessert: goat cheese, nuts and port. They present a classic combination that makes this dessert the perfect finish to any meal. *Serves 8*

CANDIED NUTS
¾ cup granulated sugar
½ cup mixed nuts (pecans, pistachios and pine nuts)
2 tsp. unsalted butter

PORT REDUCTION
1 cup ruby port
¼ cup simple syrup (page 126)

PÂTE BRISÉE (TART PASTRY)
2 cups unsalted butter, softened
⅓ cup granulated sugar
1 Tbsp. salt
5 cups pastry flour, sifted
3 egg yolks
¼ cup ice water

FILLING
1¼ cups mild goat cheese (chèvre)
½ cup granulated sugar
2 eggs
1 vanilla bean, pulp only
½ tsp. fresh lemon juice
¼ cup apricot or raspberry preserve

TO MAKE CANDIED NUTS: Melt 1 tablespoon of the sugar in a heavy-bottomed saucepan on medium-high heat. Stirring constantly, add the sugar 1 tablespoon at a time until all incorporated and light amber. Gently stir in mixed nuts and continue to cook until caramel turns dark amber. Remove from the heat and carefully stir in butter.

Line a baking sheet with aluminum foil and lightly butter it. Pour caramelized nuts onto the foil-lined baking sheet and allow to cool. When cold, break into 1-inch pieces. Store in an airtight container; will keep for up to 1 week.

PORT REDUCTION: Combine port and simple syrup in a saucepan on high heat and bring to a boil. Cook until reduced by half, or until it reaches a syrup-like consistency. Allow to cool. Place in a covered container and refrigerate until ready to use.

PÂTE BRISÉE: Place butter, sugar and salt in a kitchen mixer with a paddle attachment and cream together until light and fluffy. On a slow speed, add pastry flour, a little at a time, until mixture reaches a mealy texture.

In another bowl, lightly whisk together egg yolks and ice water. With kitchen mixer on slow speed, gradually add egg mixture to flour mixture, until just mixed. Do not overmix.

Turn out dough onto a lightly floured surface and knead gently for 1 minute. Form into a log shape and wrap tightly in plastic wrap. Refrigerate for 2 hours.

Butter and lightly flour eight 4-inch diameter tart shell molds. On a floured surface, roll out eight pastry rounds about 6 inches in diameter and ⅛ inch thick. Lightly press dough into tart shell molds. Use a fork to pierce dough in the bottom of each shell five or six times. Refrigerate for 20 minutes. (Leftover dough will keep in the freezer for up to 1 month.)

Preheat the oven to 350°F.

Cut eight squares of cheesecloth, 6 × 6 inches, just big enough to cover the bottom of a tart. Line each tart shell with a piece of cheesecloth, then fill with dried beans, about 1 cup per tart shell, to prevent bubbles from forming. Place tart molds on a baking sheet and bake in the oven for 10 to 12 minutes, or until dough in the bottom feels dry. Remove from the oven, then remove the dried beans and cheesecloth. (Do not discard beans as they can be used repeatedly.) Allow tart shells, still in their molds, to cool on a baking rack.

FILLING: Cream together goat cheese and sugar in a kitchen mixer with a paddle attachment until light in colour.

In a bowl, lightly beat eggs with vanilla bean pulp. (Save vanilla bean pod for another use.) At low speed, add egg mixture a little at a time to cheese mixture, scraping edges down periodically. Increase speed to medium and beat for 1 minute to increase volume. Stir in lemon juice. Strain through a fine-mesh sieve.

TO ASSEMBLE: Place the pastry shells, still in their molds, on a baking sheet. Brush the insides of each shell with a little fruit preserve to seal the pastry. Fill each tart to the top with goat cheese filling. Bake in the oven for about 10 minutes, or until filling sets (the sides will be slightly raised). Remove from the oven and allow to cool.

TO SERVE: Remove tarts from their molds and place in the centre of each of eight dessert plates. Drizzle 1 tablespoon of port reduction around each tart and top with 1 tablespoon candied mixed nuts.

PASSION FRUIT *Soufflé* WITH *Chocolate* SAUCE

S _oufflés are known for being tempera-_
mental, but don't let that intimidate
you. One tip is to make sure that the bowl
in which you are whipping your egg whites
is spotless. This is an easy recipe, and
one that you can make ahead of time and
freeze in individual ramekins. If you pre-
freeze the soufflés, just take them out of
the freezer and put them into the refrigerator to rest for 1 hour. Then bake, serve—
and impress all of your friends. *Serves 4 or 8*

SAUCE

1 cup heavy cream
6 oz. bittersweet dark chocolate,
   finely chopped

PASTRY CREAM

1 cup milk
3 egg yolks
½ cup granulated sugar
¼ cup all-purpose flour

SOUFFLÉ

⅓ cup passion fruit purée
   (specialty stores)
1 orange, zest only
5 egg whites
3 Tbsp. granulated sugar
Icing sugar for dusting

TO MAKE SAUCE: Place cream in a
saucepan on medium heat and bring just
to a boil. Remove from the heat.

Place chocolate in a bowl, then pour
warm cream over it, whisking until smooth.
Allow to cool. Cover and refrigerate until
ready to use.

PASTRY CREAM: Heat milk in a saucepan
on medium heat, and bring just to a boil.
Strain milk through a fine-mesh sieve.

Whisk together egg yolks and sugar in
a bowl for about 2 minutes. Whisk in flour.
Temper the egg mixture by whisking in
some of the warm milk. Slowly add the rest
of the milk, whisking until smooth.

Transfer mixture to a clean saucepan
on medium heat and bring to a boil. Cook
for about 2 to 3 minutes, whisking constantly, until it softens slightly and will coat
the back of a spoon. Remove from the
heat and strain through a fine-mesh sieve
to remove any lumps. Cover with plastic
wrap, gently pressing down on the surface
to prevent a skin from forming. Allow to
cool. (Will keep in an airtight container in
the refrigerator for up to 2 days.)

SOUFFLÉ: Preheat the oven to 425°F.

Whisk passion fruit purée and orange zest into the pastry cream.

Whisk egg whites in a kitchen mixer on medium speed while gradually adding sugar. Continue to whisk until egg whites form stiff peaks. Fold a quarter of egg white mixture into the passion fruit mixture, then gently fold in the remaining egg whites.

Spoon soufflé mixture into buttered and sugared ramekins: eight of them 3 inches in diameter, or four of them 6 inches in diameter. Run your thumb around the edge of each ramekin to remove excess batter on the rim. This will ensure that the soufflés rise evenly.

Place the ramekins in a baking pan and fill the pan with boiling water to reach halfway up the sides of the ramekins. Bake in the oven for 12 to 15 minutes, or until golden brown on top. Remove from the oven.

TO ASSEMBLE: Reheat the chocolate sauce in a double boiler on medium-low heat or in a microwave on medium for 30 seconds, stirring occasionally until heated through. If too thick, add a little milk (or cream).

Dust tops of soufflés with icing sugar. Place the ramekins on individual napkin-lined plates. Serve warm chocolate sauce in a pitcher on the side.

Blackberries IN MOSCATO WITH LEMON VERBENA ANGLAISE, VANILLA CREAM AND *Lime Zest* WAFER

The best time to make this dessert is in late summer, when the blackberries are at the height of their season, all ripe and plump and juicy. The verbena complements the floral soapiness of the berries and the Moscato adds a surprising and pleasant effervescence.

Fresh blackberries are so good you can even serve them on their own, with just a bit of lemon or lime zest and a touch of sugar. *Serves 4*

BLACKBERRIES

4 cups blackberries, fresh or frozen
   and thawed
1 cup Moscato
3 Tbsp. granulated sugar
½ vanilla bean, split and scraped
Squeeze of fresh lemon juice

LEMON VERBENA ANGLAISE

½ cup heavy cream
½ cup light cream or half-and-half
¼ cup granulated sugar
¼ cup lemon verbena
3 egg yolks

VANILLA CREAM

¾ cup heavy cream
1 Tbsp. granulated sugar
½ vanilla bean, pulp only
¼ cup mascarpone

WAFERS

½ cup unsalted butter, softened
1¼ cups granulated sugar
1 vanilla bean, pulp only
1 egg
1 egg yolk
1 tsp. fresh lime juice
1 Tbsp. fine lime zest
¾ cup all-purpose flour, sifted
Icing sugar for dusting

TO MAKE BLACKBERRIES: Combine 1 cup of the blackberries, Moscato, sugar, vanilla bean pulp and pod, and lemon juice in a saucepan on medium heat. Bring to a boil, then decrease the heat to medium-low and simmer until berries are very soft. Remove from the heat and allow to cool for 15 minutes.

Purée in a food processor or blender. Strain through a fine-mesh sieve into a clean saucepan on medium-low heat. Gently simmer for 5 minutes. Remove from the heat and allow to cool.

Add the remaining blackberries to cooled purée and mix very gently to coat them. Allow to marinate for at least 1 hour at room temperature before serving.

ANGLAISE: Combine heavy cream, light cream (or half-and-half), half of the sugar and lemon verbena in a saucepan on medium heat and bring to just a boil. Remove from the heat and allow to infuse for at least 30 minutes.

Whisk together egg yolks and the remaining sugar in a bowl until light and fluffy. Temper egg mixture by whisking in a small amount of the warm infused cream, then slowly add the rest of the cream.

Strain through a fine-mesh sieve into a clean saucepan on medium heat, stirring constantly with a wooden spoon. Bring to 175°F on a candy thermometer, or until the mixture coats the back of the spoon. Do not boil or overcook, as it will curdle.

Remove from the heat and immediately strain through a fine-mesh sieve into a clean stainless steel bowl placed on a bowl of ice to stop the cooking. Allow to cool, then cover and refrigerate until ready to use. Will keep in the refrigerator for up to 2 days.

VANILLA CREAM: Place cream, sugar and vanilla bean pulp in a chilled stainless steel bowl and whip until stiff peaks form. (Save vanilla bean pod for another use.)

In another bowl, lightly whisk mascarpone. Fold mascarpone into the whipped vanilla cream. Cover and refrigerate until ready to use. Will keep for up to 2 days.

WAFERS: Cream together butter, sugar and vanilla bean pulp in the bowl of a kitchen mixer with a paddle attachment on medium-high speed until light and fluffy.

In another bowl, lightly whisk together egg and egg yolk. On a low speed, add beaten eggs to butter mixture. Add lime juice and lime zest. Slowly add flour, mixing until fully incorporated. Cover and refrigerate until ready to use. (Batter may be made ahead up to this point. Will keep in the refrigerator for 5 days or in the freezer for 1 month.)

Preheat the oven to 325°F.

Drop the wafer batter, 1 teaspoon at time, onto a parchment-lined baking sheet. Place the drops about 3 inches apart as they will spread when baked. Bake in the oven for 4 to 6 minutes, or until edges are golden brown.

TO ASSEMBLE: Drizzle 2 tablespoons of crème anglaise in the centre of each of four bowls or dessert plates. Use a slotted spoon to pick up ¾ cup of drained blackberries per serving and place on top of the crème anglaise. Place a dollop of vanilla cream on each serving of blackberries and top with a lime zest wafer. Dust a little icing sugar over the wafers.

BABY *Banana* IN SHREDDED PHYLLO WITH
Coconut-CHOCOLATE ICE CREAM

I believe this is one of my favourite desserts that we have ever created, either in the restaurant or the bar. The combination of coconut, chocolate and bananas is a bit different but a very natural one, and delicious. Although it is a little messy to make, it's easy. And fun. *Serves 6*

COCONUT-CHOCOLATE ICE CREAM

½ cup heavy cream
½ cup milk
1 cup coconut purée (specialty stores)
5 egg yolks
½ cup granulated sugar
½ cup dark chocolate, ¼-inch pieces

BANANAS

4 Tbsp. fresh lemon juice
1 Tbsp. simple syrup (page 126)
1 Tbsp. ground cinnamon
6 baby bananas
¼ to ½ pkg. frozen shredded phyllo, thawed
1 cup unsalted butter, melted
⅓ cup honey
Icing sugar for dusting

TO MAKE ICE CREAM: Combine cream, milk and coconut purée in a saucepan on medium heat and bring to just to a boil. Remove from the heat and allow to infuse for 5 minutes.

Whisk together egg yolks and sugar in a bowl, until light and fluffy. Temper the egg mixture by whisking in a small amount of the warm coconut mixture, then slowly add the rest of the coconut while whisking constantly.

Strain through a fine-mesh sieve into a clean saucepan and return to the heat, stirring constantly with a wooden spoon. Cook until mixture reads 175°F on a candy thermometer or mixture coats the back of the spoon. Do not boil or overcook, as it will curdle.

Remove from the heat and strain through a fine-mesh sieve into a stainless steel bowl placed over a bowl of ice to stop the cooking. Allow to cool. Cover and refrigerate for 1 to 2 hours.

Melt chocolate over a double boiler on medium-low heat and keep warm.

Place the coconut mixture in an ice-cream maker and process according to the manufacturer's instructions. When it looks almost frozen (three quarters done), pour the melted chocolate in a steady drizzle into the ice cream as it is churning. (When the warm chocolate hits the cold ice cream, it will turn into shards that will break down into little pieces during the churning.) Finish churning ice cream until it is frozen. Freeze overnight before serving. Makes about 2 cups. Will keep in the freezer for up to 1 month.

continued overleaf >

BANANAS: Preheat the oven to 325°F.

Mix together lemon juice, simple syrup and ground cinnamon in a bowl until they form a thin paste. Peel bananas and coat well with cinnamon mixture.

Spread shredded phyllo thinly on a clean working surface to form a rectangle 24 × 6 inches (the long side should be at the bottom).

Mix together warm melted butter and honey in a bowl. Drizzle half of the butter mixture over shredded phyllo and dust with icing sugar. Place bananas in a line along the bottom of the phyllo rectangle, then cut phyllo into pieces that are ½ inch wider than the length of each banana. Tightly roll up each banana in phyllo, place on a parchment-lined baking sheet and drizzle with the remaining butter mixture.

Bake in the oven for 8 to 10 minutes, then turn over and continue to bake for another 8 to 10 minutes, or until dark golden brown. Remove from the oven and trim off the rough ends of the rolls.

TO ASSEMBLE: Dust the phyllo-wrapped bananas with icing sugar, cut in half and place both halves in the centre of each of six plates. Place a scoop of coconut-chocolate ice cream on the side.

RICE *Pudding* WITH VANILLA-STEWED RHUBARB

When rhubarb is in season, be sure to pick thin stalks that are a deep pinky red in colour and with as few imperfections as possible. There is nothing finer than eating stewed rhubarb. It's something my mother made all the time. We used to simply eat stewed rhubarb on its own or over vanilla ice cream, but after trying it with the creaminess of this rice pudding, it is hard to think of eating it any other way. *Serves 8*

RICE PUDDING

1 cup good quality arborio rice
1 cup granulated sugar
1 cup water
1 vanilla bean, split and pulp scraped
4 cups milk
2 cups heavy cream

RHUBARB

1 lb. thin stalks rhubarb
½ cup granulated sugar
2 Tbsp. water
½ vanilla bean, split and pulp scraped
½ lemon, juice of

TO MAKE RICE PUDDING: Combine rice, sugar, water, vanilla bean pulp and pod, and milk in a heavy-bottomed saucepan on medium-high heat and bring just to a boil. Decrease the heat to medium-low and, stirring occasionally, simmer for about 15 minutes until rice has plumped out and you can just see the rice under the milky surface.

Add cream, increase the heat to medium-high and bring back to a boil. Decrease the heat to medium-low and, stirring occasionally, gently simmer for about 10 minutes, or until you can see the rice under the surface of the cream. Remove from the heat and allow to cool for 30 minutes, stirring from time to time. Remove and discard vanilla pod. Cover and refrigerate until needed; will keep in an airtight container for up to 3 days.

RHUBARB: Cut rhubarb into 2-inch pieces. Combine rhubarb, sugar, water, and vanilla bean pulp and pod in a saucepan on medium heat and bring to a boil. Decrease the heat to low and simmer for about 15 minutes, or until rhubarb is tender. Remove from the heat and stir in lemon juice. Allow to cool. Remove and discard vanilla pod. Cover and refrigerate until ready to use; will keep in an airtight container for up to 3 days.

TO ASSEMBLE: Bring rice pudding to room temperature or warm gently on the stove-top or in a microwave on medium for 45 seconds, or until lukewarm. Divide rice pudding among eight dessert bowls and arrange stewed rhubarb on the top.

The Basics

CHICKEN STOCK

5 lbs. fresh chicken bones, backs and
    necks
1 large carrot, coarsely chopped
1 medium leek, white part only, finely
    chopped
1 medium onion, coarsely chopped
2 stalks celery, coarsely chopped
5 cloves garlic
2 sprigs fresh thyme
2 bay leaves

Rinse chicken bones, backs and necks thoroughly under cold running water for 5 to 10 minutes, or until water runs clear. Cut off and discard fatty skin. Place chicken in a large stockpot and cover with cold water. On medium heat, bring to a boil. Decrease the heat to low and simmer, uncovered, for 20 minutes, frequently skimming off and discarding the fat and impurities that rise to the surface.

Add all remaining ingredients and simmer, uncovered, on low heat, for 2 hours. To ensure a clear stock, do not allow to boil. Frequently skim off and discard fat and impurities that rise to the top.

Remove from the heat and strain through a fine-mesh sieve into a clean container. Allow to cool. Cover and refrigerate. Once the stock has been refrigerated for a few hours, the fat rises to the top and hardens, making it easy to remove and discard.

Can be used right away. Will keep in the refrigerator for up to 4 days or in the freezer for up to 2 months.

Makes about 16 cups

DARK CHICKEN STOCK

3 lbs. fresh chicken backs, necks and a
    few wings
3 Tbsp. vegetable oil
1 medium carrot, coarsely chopped
1 medium onion, coarsely chopped
2 cloves garlic, halved
1 stalk celery, coarsely chopped
3 sprigs fresh thyme
2 bay leaves
10 whole black peppercorns

Preheat the oven to 450°F.

Rinse chicken backs, necks and wings thoroughly under cold running water for 5 to 10 minutes, or until water runs clear. Cut off and discard fatty skin.

Heat vegetable oil in a large roasting pan on high heat. Add chicken pieces and roast in the oven for about 45 minutes, or until light brown. It's very important to make sure the chicken does not burn, or the stock will taste bitter.

Add carrot, onion, garlic and celery. Place back in the oven for another 30 minutes, or until bones turn dark brown and vegetables are caramelized. Pour off and discard fat.

Transfer roasted bones and vegetables to a stockpot on the stove-top on medium heat. Add a little cold water and stir to deglaze the bottom of the pan. Pour into the stockpot

Add enough cold water to the stockpot to cover chicken bones and vegetables. Add thyme, bay leaves and peppercorns. Increase the heat to high and bring to a boil. Decrease the heat to medium-low and gently simmer for 3 to 4 hours, or until rich golden brown. Frequently skim off and discard fat and impurities that rise to the top.

Remove from the heat and strain stock through a fine-mesh sieve into a clean container and allow to cool. Discard solids. Stock can be used as is, but for more intense flavour, reduce by half on low heat.

Can be used right away. Will keep in the refrigerator for up to 4 days or in the freezer for up to 2 months.

Makes about 8 cups, or 4 cups reduced

MUSHROOM STOCK

2 Tbsp. vegetable oil
2 lbs. mushroom trimmings
2 cloves garlic, peeled
3 sprigs fresh thyme
2 large shallots, peeled and finely sliced
4 cups water or chicken stock (page 120)

Preheat the oven to 375°F.

Heat vegetable oil in a stockpot on medium-high heat. Sauté mushroom trimmings, garlic, thyme and shallots, until mushrooms are very soft. Add water (or stock). Bring to a boil, then decrease the heat to medium-low and simmer for 30 minutes.

Remove from the heat and strain through a fine-mesh sieve, lightly pressing solids to extract as much liquid as possible. For more intense flavour, reduce by one third on low heat.

Can be used right away. Will keep in the refrigerator for up to 1 week or in the freezer for up to 2 months.

Makes about 4 cups, or 2⅔ cups reduced

VEGETABLE STOCK

1 bulb fennel, thinly sliced
1 medium onion, peeled and thinly sliced
2 stalks celery, thinly sliced
1 medium carrot, thinly sliced
1 leek, thinly sliced
1 tomato, roughly chopped
4 cloves garlic, peeled
1 tsp. whole white peppercorns
3 sprigs thyme
1-inch piece fresh ginger, sliced
5 cups water

Combine all ingredients in a stockpot on medium heat and bring to a boil. Decrease the heat to low and simmer for 30 to 45 minutes. Frequently skim off and discard impurities that rise to the top.

Remove from the heat and strain through a fine-mesh sieve, lightly pressing solids to extract as much liquid as possible.

Can be used right away. Will keep in the refrigerator for up to 1 week or in the freezer for up to 2 months.

Makes about 4 cups

VEAL STOCK

1 lb. milk-fed veal bones (shank if possible)

⅓ cup honey

⅓ cup unsalted butter

1 medium carrot, coarsely chopped

1 leek, white part only, coarsely chopped

½ medium onion, peeled and chopped

1 stalk celery, coarsely chopped

5 cloves garlic, peeled and minced

1 Tbsp. tomato paste

1 tomato, peeled, seeded and chopped

2 sprigs fresh thyme

1 bay leaf

Preheat the oven to 450°F.

Place bones in a large roasting pan and roast in the oven for 30 to 35 minutes, or until lightly browned. Pour off and discard excess fat from the pan, then roast bones for another 10 minutes.

Melt honey and butter in a saucepan on medium heat. Pour honey mixture over bones and roast for another 5 minutes. Transfer bones to a large stockpot and set aside. Leave the oven on.

Place carrot, leek, onion, celery and garlic in the same roasting pan in which you roasted the bones. Roast vegetables in the oven or cook on medium-high heat on the stove-top for about 10 minutes, or until golden brown. Add 2 cups cold water and bring to a boil, stirring to deglaze the bottom of the pan. Cook until reduced by half. Add to bones in the stockpot. Add tomato paste, tomato, thyme and bay leaf.

Add enough cold water to cover bones. On low heat, simmer for 6 to 8 hours (do not allow to boil). Frequently skim off and discard fat and impurities that rise to the top. Keep the stock ingredients at least three quarters covered with water, adding more cold water as needed.

Remove from the heat and allow to cool slightly. Strain through a fine-mesh sieve into a clean container; discard solids but reserve bones (see Remoulage below).

Can be used right away. Will keep in the refrigerator for up to 1 week or in the freezer for up to 3 months.

Makes about 5 cups

REMOULAGE

After you have prepared your veal stock, don't throw away the cooked bones. They will still have some flavour, enough for a *remoulage*, or a second extraction of veal stock. You can use the remoulage for a base instead of cold water for your next veal stock.

Preheat the oven to 450°F. Prepare half the quantity of vegetables called for in the veal stock recipe and toss with ¼ cup vegetable oil in a roasting pan. Roast in the oven for about 10 minutes, or until golden brown. Add a little water and stir to deglaze the bottom of the pan.

Transfer to a stockpot, add bones and cover with cold water. Bring to a boil on medium-high, then decrease the heat to low and simmer for 45 minutes. Frequently skim off and discard fat and impurities that rise to the top.

Remove from the heat and strain through a fine-mesh sieve into a clean container; discard vegetables and bones.

Can be used right away. Will keep in the refrigerator for up to 1 week or in the freezer for up to 3 months.

Makes about 4 cups

VEAL REDUCTION

¾ cup dry red wine, such as a Shiraz-
    Cabernet blend
⅓ cup ruby port
½ cup shallots, peeled and finely sliced
¼ head garlic, cut in half
2 sprigs fresh thyme
5 cups good quality veal stock

Combine red wine and port in a stockpot on medium heat. Add shallots, garlic and thyme, then cook until liquid is reduced to a syrup. Add stock and cook until reduced by one third.

Remove from the heat and strain through a fine-mesh sieve into a clean container and allow to cool.

Can be used right away. Will keep in the refrigerator for up to 1 week or in the freezer for up to 3 months.

Makes about 3 cups

LAMB OR BEEF STOCK

See also short stock on page 124.
2 lbs. lamb or beef bones
3 medium carrots, cut in chunks
2 medium onions, cut in chunks
4 stalks celery, cut in chunks
1 head garlic, cut in half
5 sprigs fresh thyme
1 bay leaf
10 black peppercorns

Preheat the oven to 450°F.

Lightly grease two roasting pans with a bit of vegetable oil. Arrange bones in a single layer in one pan and roast in the oven, turning occasionally, for 1 to 1½ hours, or until dark brown. At the same time, place carrots, onions, celery and garlic in the other pan and roast in the oven for 45 to 60 minutes, or until caramelized. Remove bones and vegetables from the oven when done.

Pour off and discard fat from the pan of bones. Place both pans on the stove-top on medium heat. Add a little water to both pans and stir to deglaze the bottoms.

Transfer the contents of both pans to a stockpot. Add thyme, bay leaf and peppercorns. Add enough cold water to cover ingredients. On medium heat, simmer, uncovered, for 3 to 4 hours. Frequently skim off and discard impurities that rise to the surface. Keep the stock ingredients at least three quarters covered with water, adding more cold water as needed. Remove from the heat and allow to cool slightly.

Strain through a fine-mesh sieve into a clean container. For more intense flavour, cook over low heat until stock is reduced by half. Cool to room temperature and refrigerate. Remove and discard the cap of fat on the stock.

Can be used right away. Will keep in the refrigerator for up to 1 week or in the freezer for up to 3 months.

Makes 8 to 10 cups, or 4 to 5 cups reduced

SHORT STOCK

2 tsp. vegetable oil

4 oz. lamb or beef trimmings, fat removed

1 medium carrot, cut in chunks

½ medium onion, cut in chunks

2 stalks celery, cut in chunks

3 cloves garlic

2 sprigs fresh thyme

1 bay leaf

2 cups veal stock (page 122)

¼ cup dry red wine, optional

If you need lamb or beef stock and do not have any on hand, you can make a fairly quick substitute by infusing veal stock with the flavour you need.

Heat vegetable oil in a large stockpot on high heat and brown meat trimmings. Drain off and discard fat. Add carrot, onion, celery, garlic, thyme and bay leaf. Cook, uncovered, stirring occasionally, until caramelized. Add stock and wine (optional), stirring to deglaze the bottom of the pan. Bring to a boil, then decrease the heat to medium-low and simmer for 1 hour. Frequently skim off and discard impurities that rise to the surface.

Strain through a fine-mesh sieve into a clean container and remove all fat. For more intense flavour, cook over low heat until reduced by half.

Makes 1½ cups, or ¾ cup reduced

TOMATO SAUCE

3 Tbsp. olive oil

4 cups finely minced onions

2 cloves garlic, minced

4 Thai chiles, deseeded and finely minced

2 Tbsp. granulated sugar

2 Tbsp. chopped fresh basil leaves

1 Tbsp. chopped fresh sage

1 Tbsp. chopped fresh thyme

3 cans whole plum tomatoes (each 28 oz.)

¼ cup extra-virgin olive oil

Heat olive oil in a large saucepan on medium heat. Sauté onions until soft and translucent. Add garlic and Thai chiles, then sauté for about 1 minute (do not brown as garlic will become bitter). Add sugar, basil, sage and thyme; continue to cook for another 3 minutes.

Crush canned tomatoes; add tomatoes and juice to the saucepan. Bring to a boil, then decrease the heat to medium-low and simmer for about 45 minutes, stirring occasionally and skimming off any impurities that rise to the surface. To finish, stir in extra-virgin olive oil. Season to taste with salt and freshly ground white pepper. Remove from the heat and allow to cool.

Can be used right away. Will keep in the refrigerator for 4 days and in the freezer for up to 2 months. For convenience, measure out and freeze in 1 or 2 cup batches.

Makes about 8 cups

TOMATO CONCASSÉ

Bring a pot of water to a boil. Add whole tomatoes and blanch them for about 10 to 20 seconds (the riper the tomatoes, the less blanching time needed). Use a slotted spoon to remove tomatoes from the boiling water and immediately plunge them into a bowl of ice water to stop the cooking. Allow tomatoes to cool for about 1 minute.

Remove tomatoes from the ice water. Use a small paring knife to remove the tomato cores, then peel. Cut tomatoes in half. Use a small spoon to gently scoop out inside flesh or gently squeeze out seeds (keep the inside flesh to make tomato sauce or to add to stocks or soups).

Cut tomatoes into ¼-inch dice; will keep in an airtight container in the refrigerator for no longer than 1 day.

INFUSED OILS

ROSEMARY OIL
1 cup fresh rosemary leaves
1½ cups fresh Italian (flat-leaf) parsley
1 cup grapeseed oil

MINT OIL
3 cups fresh mint leaves
1 cup fresh Italian (flat-leaf) parsley
1 cup grapeseed oil

CILANTRO OIL
1 cup fresh cilantro
½ cup fresh Italian (flat-leaf) parsley
1 cup grapeseed oil

PARSLEY OIL
½ cup fresh Italian (flat-leaf) parsley
1 cup grapeseed oil

For these herb oils, the ingredients are different but the cooking instructions are the same.

Blanch herbs by placing them in boiling water just till they wilt, about 10 seconds. Immediately shock herb by transferring them to a bowl of ice water to preserve colour. Drain herbs, then dry thoroughly between two towels.

Purée herbs in a blender, then slowly add grapeseed oil and incorporate. Transfer to an airtight container and refrigerate overnight to infuse. Strain through a cheesecloth-lined sieve and discard herbs.

Herb oils will keep in the refrigerator for up to 2 months in an airtight container.

Makes about 1 cup each

GARLIC PURÉE
1 Tbsp. olive oil
10 large cloves garlic, peeled
2 tsp. honey
½ cup chicken stock (page 120) or water
½ cup heavy cream

Heat olive oil in a small saucepan over medium-low heat. Gently sauté garlic until golden brown. Add honey and cook until garlic is caramelized, being careful not to burn it. Add stock (or water) and reduce until garlic is glazed and soft. Add cream and bring to a boil. Decrease the heat and simmer for 5 minutes. Remove from the heat and allow to cool for 5 minutes.

Purée in a blender or food processor and strain through a fine-mesh sieve. Place in a covered container and refrigerate until needed. Will keep in the refrigerator for up to 4 days.

Makes about ¼ cup

PRESERVED LEMONS

10 to 12 large lemons
3 Tbsp. salt
1 Tbsp. crushed coriander seeds
¼ cup honey
1 cup fresh lemon juice
3 cups warm water
3 bay leaves

Wash lemons well. Use a paring knife to make a cross-shaped cut in each lemon (as if cutting it into quarter wedges), but cut only two thirds of the way through, leaving lemon wedges still joined. These cuts will allow lemons to absorb salt and sugar while still remaining in one piece.

Lay the cut lemons on a baking sheet and place in the freezer for at least 12 hours.

Sterilize three 1-quart glass canning jars. Take lemons out of the freezer and place them, cut side up, to form one layer in the bottom of each jar. Sprinkle the cuts in lemons with some of the salt and some of the crushed coriander seeds. Repeat with another layer of lemons, salt and coriander, until jars are full.

Mix together any remaining salt with honey, lemon juice and warm water in a stainless steel bowl. Pour equal amounts of this liquid into each jar and add a bay leaf to each. Seal and can according to the manufacturer's instructions. Refrigerate for at least 6 weeks before using. Will keep in the refrigerator for up to 2 months.

When you use the preserved lemons, discard the inside flesh and use only the peel.

Makes about 4 cups

BALSAMIC GLAZE

2 cups balsamic vinegar

Place balsamic vinegar in a saucepan on medium heat and simmer until reduced to ½ cup. Remove from the heat and allow to cool. Place in an airtight glass container. Will keep in the refrigerator for up to 2 weeks.

Makes ½ cup

SIMPLE SYRUP

2 cups granulated sugar
1½ cups water

Combine sugar and water in a saucepan on medium-high heat and bring to a boil. Continue to boil for 2 minutes. Remove from the heat and strain through a fine-mesh sieve. Allow to cool. Store at room temperature in an airtight container. Will keep for up to 10 days.

Makes about 2 cups

SIMPLE SYRUP FOR COCKTAILS

2 cups granulated sugar
1 cup water

Combine sugar and water in a saucepan on medium heat and bring to a boil. Immediately remove from the heat and allow to cool. Store in a sealed container in the refrigerator, where it will keep indefinitely.

Makes about 2 cups

RENDERED DUCK OR GOOSE FAT

Never throw away duck or goose fat used in cooking, for it can be reused. Melt the fat, then strain through a fine-mesh sieve and pour into airtight containers.

4 lbs. duck or goose fat, 1-inch pieces
1 cup water

Place fat and water in a saucepan on low heat until fat melts and the water has evaporated. Remove from the heat and allow to cool for 10 minutes. Strain through a fine-mesh sieve into airtight containers. Will keep in the refrigerator for up to 3 weeks or in the freezer for up to 1 year.
Makes about 4 cups

CLARIFIED BUTTER

2 cups unsalted butter

Place butter in a double boiler over boiling water on medium-high heat. Cook until the butter separates and milk solids appear. Skim off and discard any white foam that forms on the surface. Remove from the heat and allow to cool for 10 minutes. Place in the refrigerator until butter hardens.

Use the handle of a serving spoon to make a small hole in the top of the hardened butter. Carefully pour away and discard water and milk solids.

Place clarified butter in an airtight container. Will keep in the refrigerator for up to 1 week.

To use, melt clarified butter as needed.
Makes about 1½ cups

FROMAGE BLANC

1 cup full-fat organic yogurt
1 cup cottage cheese
1½ tsp. fresh lemon juice

Purée yogurt and cottage cheese in a food processor or blender until very smooth. Add lemon juice and incorporate. Transfer to an airtight container and refrigerate for at least 24 hours before using. Will keep in the refrigerator for up to 1 week.
Makes about 2 cups

MAYONNAISE

1 egg
1 Tbsp. rice vinegar
1 tsp. fresh lemon juice
1 tsp. Dijon mustard
1 cup grapeseed oil

Combine egg, rice vinegar, lemon juice and Dijon mustard in a food processor or blender on medium speed. With the motor running, slowly drizzle in grapeseed oil in a steady stream. Transfer to an airtight container. Will keep in the refrigerator for up to 1 week.
Makes about 1 cup

TEMPURA BATTER

2 eggs

2 cups sparkling water, ice cold

2 cups rice flour

¼ tsp. salt

Whisk together eggs and sparkling water in a bowl. Add rice flour and salt, whisking until just incorporated. Will keep in the refrigerator for 1 day, but it's best to make it just before using.

Makes about 2 cups

BRIOCHE

1 Tbsp. active dry yeast

¼ cup granulated sugar

4 Tbsp. warm water

6 eggs

4 cups all-purpose flour

1 Tbsp. salt

1 vanilla bean, pulp only

2 cups unsalted butter, softened

Combine yeast with 2 tablespoons of the sugar and warm water in a bowl. Cover the bowl with plastic wrap and place it in a warm area. Allow yeast to dissolve.

In another bowl, beat eggs with the remaining sugar.

Sift flour and salt into the bowl of a kitchen mixer with a dough hook attachment. Pour in yeast mixture. Add vanilla bean pulp. (Save vanilla bean husk for another use.) On medium speed, gradually pour in egg mixture and beat until dough is smooth. Slowly add butter a little at a time, beating continually until incorporated.

Change to a paddle attachment on the kitchen mixer. On high speed, beat mixture until dough pulls away from the sides of the bowl. Place dough in an oiled bowl and cover with plastic wrap. Refrigerate for at least 4 hours.

Roll out dough on a lightly floured surface to form a cylinder long enough to fit into a bread pan but only halfway up the sides.

Butter a bread pan and place dough inside, using your fingers to gently press it to fit the shape of the pan and to flatten it on top. Place the bread pan on a baking sheet and put in a warm area to proof for 25 to 35 minutes, or until dough has doubled in bulk and the bread pan is nearly full.

Preheat the oven to 375°F.

Bake dough in the oven for 20 to 30 minutes, or until dark golden brown. The bread should sound hollow when you tap on it gently with your fingers.

Remove from the oven, take the loaf out of the bread pan and allow to cool on a rack. Use right away or wrap tightly in plastic wrap for later use. Will keep in the refrigerator for up to 4 days or in the freezer for up to 6 months.

Makes 1 loaf

RAVIOLI

14 oz. all-purpose flour

14 oz. semolina

Pinch of salt

16 large egg yolks

1 to 4 whole eggs

1½ tsp. olive oil

1 whole egg, beaten

½ tsp. water

Semolina or fine cornmeal for dusting

Place flour, semolina and salt in the bowl of a heavy-duty kitchen mixer with a dough hook. On a slow speed, incorporate egg yolks one at a time, followed by 1 whole egg. Test dough by squeezing some of the mixture in your hand. If it stays together, do not add more whole eggs. If it does not stay together, incorporate 1 more whole egg and test. Keep adding and testing 1 whole egg at a time as needed until dough is ready.

When dough is ready, add oil and knead. It should form a dough that is not too wet or too sticky. If mixture is too liquid, add more flour.

Gently knead dough on a lightly floured surface and form into two cylinders that are 3 inches thick. Cut each cylinder into four equal portions. Wrap the eight portions in plastic wrap and allow to rest in the refrigerator for 1 hour before using.

Roll out each portion of dough in a pasta machine, according to the manufacturer's instructions, to form a thin sheet about ⅟₁₆ inch thick. The sheet should be large enough to go into a ravioli mold. As the sheets of dough are rolled out, cover them with a clean cloth so they won't dry out. Make eight sheets of pasta.

Sprinkle the inside of the ravioli mold with a little flour to prevent sticking. Line the mold with one sheet of pasta, pressing gently into the spaces. Place the filling in a pastry bag with a round flat tip and pipe about 1 tablespoon into each square in the ravioli mold.

Place beaten egg and water in a bowl and whisk together to make an egg wash. Place another sheet of pasta on a clean surface. Use a pastry brush to paint one side of the sheet of pastry with egg wash. Carefully place the pastry sheet, egg wash side down, over the filled ravioli. Gently press along the seams to ensure the egg wash seals the pasta sheets together and also to get rid of any air bubbles. Use a floured rolling pin to gently roll over the top sheet. This will help to mold the individual ravioli pieces.

Trim off the outside edges and discard any trimmings. Turn over the mold onto a parchment-lined baking sheet and remove all the ravioli in one piece from the mold. Place the tray in the freezer. Repeat until all the pasta dough is used up. After being frozen, the ravioli in each mold will break apart (each mold makes 10 ravioli). No cutting is necessary if done properly.

(The ravioli can be made ahead up to this point. Place in an airtight container; will keep in the freezer for up to 2½ weeks.) Do not thaw before cooking. Place frozen ravioli in a large pot of boiling salted water and cook for about 4½ minutes, or until done.

Makes about 40 ravioli

Metric Conversions

(rounded off to nearest even whole number)

<table>
<tr><td colspan="2">WEIGHT</td><td colspan="2">VOLUME</td></tr>
<tr><td>IMPERIAL OR U.S.</td><td>METRIC</td><td>IMPERIAL OR U.S.</td><td>METRIC</td></tr>
<tr><td>1 oz.</td><td>30 g</td><td>⅛ tsp</td><td>0.5 mL</td></tr>
<tr><td>2 oz.</td><td>60 g</td><td>¼ tsp.</td><td>1 mL</td></tr>
<tr><td>3 oz.</td><td>85 g</td><td>½ tsp.</td><td>2.5 mL</td></tr>
<tr><td>4 oz.</td><td>115 g</td><td>¾ tsp.</td><td>4 mL</td></tr>
<tr><td>5 oz.</td><td>140 g</td><td>1 tsp.</td><td>5 mL</td></tr>
<tr><td>6 oz.</td><td>170 g</td><td>1 Tbsp.</td><td>15 mL</td></tr>
<tr><td>7 oz.</td><td>200 g</td><td></td><td></td></tr>
<tr><td>8 oz. (½ lb.)</td><td>225 g</td><td>⅛ cup</td><td>30 mL</td></tr>
<tr><td>9 oz.</td><td>255 g</td><td>¼ cup</td><td>60 mL</td></tr>
<tr><td>10 oz.</td><td>285 g</td><td>⅓ cup</td><td>80 mL</td></tr>
<tr><td>11 oz.</td><td>310 g</td><td>½ cup</td><td>120 mL</td></tr>
<tr><td>12 oz.</td><td>340 g</td><td>⅔ cup</td><td>160 mL</td></tr>
<tr><td>13 oz.</td><td>370 g</td><td>¾ cup</td><td>180 mL</td></tr>
<tr><td>14 oz.</td><td>400 g</td><td>1 cup</td><td>240 mL</td></tr>
<tr><td>15 oz.</td><td>425 g</td><td></td><td></td></tr>
<tr><td>1 lb. (16 oz.)</td><td>455 g</td><td colspan="2">OVEN TEMPERATURE</td></tr>
<tr><td>2 lb.</td><td>910 g</td><td>IMPERIAL OR U.S.</td><td>METRIC</td></tr>
<tr><td></td><td></td><td>250°F</td><td>120°C</td></tr>
<tr><td></td><td></td><td>275°F</td><td>135°C</td></tr>
<tr><td></td><td></td><td>300°F</td><td>150°C</td></tr>
<tr><td></td><td></td><td>325°F</td><td>160°C</td></tr>
<tr><td></td><td></td><td>350°F</td><td>180°C</td></tr>
<tr><td></td><td></td><td>375°F</td><td>190°C</td></tr>
<tr><td></td><td></td><td>400°F</td><td>200°C</td></tr>
<tr><td></td><td></td><td>425°F</td><td>220°C</td></tr>
<tr><td></td><td></td><td>450°F</td><td>230°C</td></tr>
</table>

LINEAR

IMPERIAL OR U.S.	METRIC
⅛ inch	3 mm
¼ inch	6 mm
½ inch	12 mm
¾ inch	2 cm
1 inch	2.5 cm
1¼ inches	3 cm
1½ inches	3.5 cm
1¾ inches	4.5 cm
2 inches	5 cm
3 inches	7.5 cm
4 inches	10 cm
5 inches	12.5 cm
6 inches	15 cm
7 inches	18 cm
12 inches	30 cm
24 inches	60 cm

LIQUID MEASURES (FOR DRINKS)

IMPERIAL OR U.S.	METRIC
¼ oz.	7 mL
⅓ oz.	10 mL
½ oz.	15 mL
⅔ oz.	20 mL
¾ oz.	22 mL
1 oz.	30 mL
1⅓ oz.	40 mL
1½ oz.	45 mL
2 oz.	60 mL
3 oz.	90 mL
4 oz.	120 mL
5 oz.	150 mL

BAKING UTENSILS

IMPERIAL OR U.S.	METRIC
5 × 9-inch loaf pan	2 L loaf pan
9 × 13-inch cake pan	4 L cake pan
11 × 17-inch baking sheet	30 × 45-cm baking sheet

Acknowledgements

I would like to thank the following people for their help with this book:

Marnie Coldham, who has been with Lumière from virtually day one, has given her heart to the restaurant and has helped me immensely. Not only is she a talented chef but her best attribute is her amazing self. Her ability to deal with me at stressful times should earn her a gold medal. Without her hard work, my life around the restaurant would be very difficult.

Marcia Kurbis, who is our pastry chef, has helped us to create some fabulous desserts. She has a very unique style, one that has given new life to the desserts at Lumière.

Chris Stearns, who has done a terrific job in the Lumière Tasting Bar. The dedication he puts into researching and making every cocktail has helped immeasurably with the bar's success and popularity.

Nic Neuman, who is a great person, has done an excellent job at the bar. He has worked his way up to assistant bartender and is my longest standing employee.

Joan Cross, who is our good friend, volunteered her time to help test our recipes. I cannot think of a more perfect person to undertake such a task because she pays great attention to detail and has a vast knowledge of food. She made many suggestions that we have used throughout the book.

Nathan Fong, who is my very close friend, spent many a day in the studio, styling our food to make it look stunning.

John Sherlock, Peter Cocking and Saeko Usukawa at Douglas & McIntyre, who put in many long hours to make this book better than I had hoped for.

I would also like to particularly thank Daniel Boulud for generously agreeing to write the foreword to this book. He and Michel Jacob, Johnny Letzer and Charlie Trotter have been a great influence on my culinary career. These outstanding chefs have taught me the fundamentals of French cuisine, and I am still learning from them.

Finally, a very special thank you to my entire staff, whom I like to consider as my extended family. Their hard work and dedication have made it all possible.

ROB FEENIE

lemon-mint with scallop and
prawns, 54–55
roast chicken with choucroute
and pomme purée, 66–67
rosemary oil, 125
rum caramel sauce, 99–100

sablefish, sake and maple
marinated, 58–59
sake and maple marinated
sablefish with hijiki-soy
sauce, 58–59
SALAD(S)
Ahi tuna sashimi and green
papaya, 15
asparagus with prosciutto and
Parmigiano-Reggiano, 17
duck breast, with vanilla-
poached quince and
pomegranate, 18–19
duck leg, orange-glazed, 16
micro green, 31
SANDWICH(ES)
beef dip, 31, 33
calamari, 34
Peking duck clubhouse, 36
sardines gremolata, 64
sashimi, Ahi tuna, and green
papaya salad, 15
SAUCE(S)
béchamel, 44
beef dip, 31, 33
Bolognese, 46–47
bordelaise, 80–81
chocolate, 110–11
hijiki-soy, 58
ice wine, 66
lemon, 104–05
Riesling, 66
rum caramel, 99–100
tartar, 34
tomato, 124
sauerkraut
choucroute, 66
sausages
Lumière's cassoulet, 64–75
SEAFOOD. *See also* Fish
calamari sandwich, 34
prawn compote, preserved
lemon and, 63

scallop and prawns, lemon-mint
risotto with, 54–55
soup, lemon grass and, 23–24
shepherd's pie, Lumière, 69–70
shiitake mushroom cappuccino,
26–27
short ribs
beef dip, 31–33
braised, 31–33
garnish, 58–59
pappardelle with, 49
short stock, 124
simple syrup, 126
simple syrup for cocktails, 126
sole, chanterelle and spinach casserole in white wine cream, 65
sorbet, honey buttermilk, 99–100
soufflé, passion fruit, 110–11
SOUP(S)
chicken noodle, 25
lemon grass and seafood, 23–24
shiitake mushroom cappuccino,
26–27
sour cream mousse, 91–92
soy sauce, hijiki, 58
soy vinaigrette, warm, 6
spice sachet, 66–67
spicy lemon grass and seafood
soup, 23–24
spinach casserole, sole,
chanterelle and, 65
squash and mascarpone ravioli
with truffle butter, 40–41
STOCK(S)
beef, 123, 124
chicken, 120
dark chicken, 120
lamb, 123, 124
mushroom, 121
remoulage, 122
short, 124
veal, 122, 123
vegetable, 123
sweet potato ice cream, 102–3

tangerine marmalade, honey,
84–85
tapenade, black olive, 10–11
tart, chocolate pecan phyllo,
88–89

tart, goat cheese, 108–9
tart pastry, 108–9
tartar sauce, 34
tempura batter, 128
tomato concassé, 124–25
tomato sauce, 124
torte, mushroom, 6–7
tripolini Bolognese, 46–47
truffle butter, 40–41
truffled pomme purée, 69–70
truffled raw milk Camembert with
roasted figs, 5
tuna sashimi, Ahi, and green
papaya salad, 15

vanilla cream, 112–13
vanilla-poached quince and pomegranate, 18–19
vanilla-stewed rhubarb, 117
VEAL
reduction, 123
remoulage, 123
short stock, 124
stock, 122
tripolini Bolognese, 46–47
vegetable stock, 121
vinaigrette
balsamic, 17
house, 16
pomegranate, 18
warm soy, 6

wafer, lime zest, 112
walnut risotto, endive, blue
cheese and, 52–53
white wine cream, 65

zucchini
ratatouille, 78–79